Small Arms, Big Impact: The Next Challenge of Disarmament

MICHAEL RENNER

Daniel Schwartz, *Research Intern*

Jane A. Peterson, *Editor*

WORLDWATCH PAPER 137
October 1997

FINANCIAL SUPPORT for the Institute is provided by the Nathan Cummings Foundation, the Geraldine R. Dodge Foundation, The Ford Foundation, the Foundation for Ecology and Development, The William and Flora Hewlett Foundation, W. Alton Jones Foundation, John D. and Catherine T. MacArthur Foundation, Charles Stewart Mott Foundation, The Curtis and Edith Munson Foundation, The Pew Charitable Trusts, Rasmussen Foundation, Rockefeller Brothers Fund, Rockefeller Financial Services, Summit Foundation, Turner Foundation, U.N. Population Fund, Wallace Genetic Foundation, Wallace Global Fund, Weeden Foundation, and the Winslow Foundation.

38006559

Table of Contents

Introduction 5

Wars and Privatized Violence 10

As Easy As Buying Fish in the Market 19

Lethal Harvests 27

Feeding the Habit 31

The Challenge of Shrinking Armies 41

Taking Weapons Out of Circulation 47

Adopting the "Orphans" of Arms Control 54

Notes 63

Tables and Figures

Table 1: *Private Security, Public Police, and Military Forces,*
 Selected Countries, Late 1980s, Early 1990s 17

Table 2: *Estimated Number of Uncleared Landmines, Most Affected*
 Countries, Relative to Population and Territory, 1997 28

Table 3: *Selected Examples of Commodities-for-Arms Transactions,*
 1980s–90s 34

Table 4: *Selected Examples of Arms Transfers from Hotspot to*
 Hotspot, 1980s–90s 40

Table 5: *Demobilizations of Soldiers in Selected Developing Countries,*
 Late 1980s and 1990s 43

Table 6: *U.N. Peacekeeping and Small-Arms Disarmament, Late 1980s*
 and 1990s 50

Table 7: *Selected Examples of Gun-Buyback Programs, 1990s* 53

Figure 1: *Number of Armed Conflicts, 1946–95* 13

Figure 2: *Deaths in Armed Conflicts, by 5-Year Period, 1946–95* 15

Figure 3: *U.S. Firearms Production, 1946–95* 23

ACKNOWLEDGMENTS: I sincerely thank Michael Klare of Hampshire College, whose pioneering work has been critical in prompting growing numbers of researchers to investigate the impact of small arms, and Phyllis Bennis of the Institute for Policy Studies, for reviewing an earlier draft of this paper. Similarly, I am grateful to all of my Worldwatch colleagues for their comments. Among them, I am particularly indebted to Christopher Flavin and David Malin Roodman for suggestions that made the final product much stronger than it otherwise would have been. Daniel Schwartz provided critical research support, fulfilling requests for data and other information with little lead time and uncovered hard-to-find materials. Jane Peterson's gentle but insistent style made the editing process a real pleasure. With Daniel in Toronto, Canada, Jane in Alexandria, Virginia, and me ensconced in New York City and rural Long Island, completing this paper testified to the possibilities of cooperating on a project over long distances with the help of telephones, fax machines, and e-mail. Despite a heavy workload, Liz Doherty turned messy manuscript pages into polished page proofs with blistering speed. Last, but not least, I would like to express my appreciation to the Worldwatch communications team—Jim Perry, Denise Byers Thomma, Mary Caron, and Amy Warehime—for making the outreach process a productive and enjoyable experience.

MICHAEL RENNER joined the Worldwatch Institute staff in 1987 and is currently a Senior Researcher. He is the author of several Worldwatch Papers, including *Budgeting for Disarmament: The Costs of War and Peace* (November 1994), and of *Fighting for Survival: Environmental Decline, Social Conflict, and the New Age of Insecurity*, published by W.W. Norton in 1996. Renner has been a co-author of Worldwatch's annual *State of the World* reports since 1989 and currently serves as associate project director for the Institute's other annual, *Vital Signs*. He holds degrees in international relations and political science from the Universities of Amsterdam, Netherlands, and Konstanz, Germany.

Introduction

A March 1997 news photograph showed a group of five casually dressed young men, gathered for a game of pool in the southern Albanian town of Memaliaj. Engrossed in choosing the best angle for shooting the next ball, the five seemed oblivious to a detail that would have captured any outsider's attention: one of them was using an assault rifle as a pool cue. But it is not only Albania, in the grip of widespread anarchy, where assault rifles and other so-called "small arms and light weapons" are now easily available in such abundance that they seem like casual accessories. As the spread of arms that can be carried by an individual has become commonplace, it has encouraged a habitual recourse to violence that threatens the cohesion and wellbeing of many societies.[1]

Less than a decade ago, newspaper articles and TV programs dealing with issues of conflict and security were dominated by images of the gleaming nuclear-tipped missiles that the two superpowers deployed in their deadly confrontation, or by the dazzling high-tech jet fighters and "smart" bombs used by the United States against Iraq. But although the firepower, reach, and precision-targeting of such major weapons systems dwarf the capacities of assault rifles and other small arms, the hundreds of millions of these low-tech, inexpensive, sturdy, and easy-to-use weapons now spread around the world are the tools for most of the killing in contemporary conflicts—causing as much as 90 percent of the deaths. Though these weapons are small in caliber, they are big, indeed devastating, in their impact.[2]

Although the information available is still sparse, mounting evidence indicates that the quantities involved are enormous. For example, there may be about 500 million military-style firearms, in addition to many hundreds of millions of guns designed for police forces or for civilian use. In some countries, including such dissimilar ones as Mozambique and the United States, there are probably as many firearms as there are people, or more. In only a few nations, including Japan and some European countries, do strict regulations and societal norms tightly limit the numbers of small arms.[3]

The rising tide of small arms poses a serious threat. Fed by essentially unrestrained production of millions, if not tens of millions, of small arms annually, public and private arsenals continue to swell. Because small arms are long-lived, they may stay in circulation for decades.

Although governments may profess concern about private arms smugglers and "rogue" suppliers such as insurgent groups or drug traffickers, they themselves are by far the most important source of those weapons. The United States and the former Soviet Union in particular have spread arms of all calibers across the planet. Given the plethora of legal and illegal trading networks for small arms, once the weapons are produced, there is virtually no telling under whose control they will end up. In fact, the original suppliers have come to be haunted by a boomerang effect, with weapons intended for friendly recipients often falling into the hands of adversaries.

A flourishing trade in secondhand arms keeps them moving from place to place. Now that the Cold War is over, armies in North America, Europe, and the former Soviet Union are shrinking; much of their excess equipment is given away or sold cheaply to other countries. And weapons left over at the end of civil wars often enter the black market and resurface in new hotspots as big parts of government armies and insurgent forces are demobilized. Arms originally supplied to combatants in Nicaragua and El Salvador, for instance, have found their way into Colombia and other parts of Latin America.

Possession of a variety of small arms is widespread in many countries, filtering far beyond armies and police forces to opposition groups, criminal organizations, private security forces, vigilante squads, and individual citizens. Indeed, it may not be much of an exaggeration to say that we are witnessing an era in which, in a sense, armies are disarming while civilians are rearming. Civilians have of course long been able to purchase weapons designed for hunting or personal protection, but lately they have been able to acquire arms that were designed for military use. This is particularly true in countries such as Angola, where governments distributed large amounts of arms to citizens in the course of civil wars.[4]

The proliferation of arms within countries has contributed to rising violence. Some countries are plagued by full-scale civil wars and others by near-wars; yet others may experience less organized violence, but are exposed to lawlessness and rising crime. Whatever the specific situation, the conviction that personal or societal problems can be resolved through the barrel of a gun seems to have adherents in many countries.

Although weapons are often acquired to provide a sense of security, the outcome may be the exact opposite. If security—for a state, a community, or an individual—is to be obtained by reliance on firepower, then one can never have enough of it. It is not surprising then that some countries endure the domestic equivalent of an arms race. But the more heavily armed a society is, the more insecure it may come to feel. The United States, for instance, has by far the strongest military in the world and the largest number of firearms circulating among the general population, yet many people are afraid to venture outside their homes at night.

The spread of small arms within society poses a particular challenge for countries emerging from long years of debilitating warfare, including several in Central America and southern Africa. These countries are striving to escape a culture of violence and consolidate a hard-won peace that still rests on shaky foundations. Contending with limited economic opportunities, they find that discontent is strong and crime is rising. Demobilized ex-combatants in particular face an uphill struggle because most of them have little civilian experience. Barely scraping by, they may be tempted to turn to banditry instead.

The proliferation of small arms is the fuel of conflict, not the starter. Widespread unemployment, poverty, social inequity, and the pressures of environmental degradation and resource depletion in the presence of large quantities of small arms make a highly combustible combination. In particular, the uncertain prospects that many young people face securing a job and establishing themselves in society may trigger deviant or even criminal behavior, feed discontent that may erupt in street riots, or foment political extremism. In general, desperate people whose hopes have worn thin are more likely to turn to violent "solutions." While the conditions tend to be much harsher in poor developing countries, this observation holds as true for an inner-city resident of Los Angeles, California, as it does for a demobilized soldier in Maputo, Mozambique. Under such circumstances, making firearms available is like lighting a match near a fuel tank.[5]

Now, thanks largely to the efforts of grassroots groups, the proliferation of small arms is beginning to attract the attention of policymakers. Dealing with small-arms proliferation will no doubt prove to be an enormous challenge. Still, there are many ways in which this problem can be addressed—assuming sufficient political will.

Since small arms are already widely dispersed, an immediate task is to reduce the quantities in circulation. This can be done by setting up programs to buy back arms from individuals and—in countries emerging from warfare— by boosting the ability of peacekeeping operations to disarm ex-combatants. To reduce what is now a virtually unencumbered flow of weapons, national export controls will need to be tightened to clamp down on illicit arms trade, and a "code of conduct" adopted to govern those transfers authorized by governments.

There is more to policies stemming small-arms proliferation than simply reducing the number of weapons. On the demand side, the quality of programs to help former soldiers make the transition to civilian life can be much improved; if designed and implemented properly and provided with adequate resources, there will be less incentive for these individuals to turn to crime and violence to make a living. Unless war-torn societies receive sufficient outside assistance to consolidate peace, the harsh living conditions in these countries may prove fertile ground for ongoing violence. Elsewhere, too, gun-control efforts will be doomed if they are not accompanied by policies to alleviate the adverse social and economic conditions that can lead to violent breakdown.

There is still a widespread presumption among policymakers that unrestrained production of small arms makes sense—to outfit police and security forces, to provide arms for personal protection, or to reap profits from selling them. A narrow cost-benefit analysis may suggest continuing with business as usual. But a comprehensive balance sheet must weigh the perceived benefits against the real costs: the loss of life and property, the climate of fear and pervasive instability, the disruption of economic development, and the threat to democratic governance that result from the violence made possible by wide availability of small arms.

If the international community is to counter the repercussions of small-arms proliferation, it will need to go beyond efforts to limit the trade and circulation of arms and move to sharply curtail future production. Because arms-control efforts have typically been limited to addressing the possession or deployment of weapons, adopting restraints on production is a notion foreign to most policymakers. Thus it is not surprising that only a handful of weapons over the past century, including chemical weapons, have been outlawed.

Still, with regard to one category of small arms—antipersonnel landmines—the idea of a ban on production has been embraced by a rapidly growing number of governments. One of the lessons of the landmines debate is that taking steps to restrict the numbers of weapons is possible only if their easy availability is seen as more of a burden than a benefit. To generate the driving force of public pressure that is necessary to move toward restraints on future production, the challenge is to dramatize the devastating impacts of assault rifles and other small weapons.

Wars and Privatized Violence

Small arms are the weapons of choice in today's typical conflict—fighting that rages within, rather than between, countries. The wide availability of these weapons is contributing to both the intensity and the duration of conflicts. Indeed, the protagonists in these conflicts are usually able to procure and stockpile enough weapons to sustain the fighting even when the international community adopts an embargo on arms deliveries, as it did against Bosnia and Rwanda, for example.[6]

What are small arms? The term "small arms and light weapons" is not easily defined, but usually includes weapons that can be carried by an individual. This class of weapons encompasses such items as pistols and revolvers, rifles and assault rifles, hand grenades, machine guns, light mortars, and light anti-tank weapons like grenade launchers and recoilless rifles. Another important category is anti-personnel landmines (which are not carried around but can easily be transported and handled by an individual). Because they are portable, shoulder-fired surface-to-air missiles are also included, even though they are far more high-tech and complex than most other small arms. The term therefore covers a broad spectrum, from weapons with exclusive military application, to firearms used by police forces, to handguns or hunting rifles in the legitimate possession of civilians.[7]

For a variety of reasons, small weapons are much harder to track and control than the major weapons systems—tanks, jets, missiles, artillery, and so forth—that so far have received the most attention from policymakers:

- Because small weapons do not carry nearly as large a price tag as big-ticket military items, their importance is all too easily underestimated. Worldwide, perhaps $3 billion worth of small arms and light weapons are being shipped across international borders each year (due to the lack of reliable data, this is just a rough estimate); that would be equivalent to about one eighth of all international arms sales.[8]

- The relatively low cost of most small arms also means that they are affordable to many sub-state groups. For just $50 million—roughly the cost of a single modern jet fighter—one can equip a small army with some 200,000 assault rifles at today's "fire-sale" prices.[9]

- Unlike major weapons, small arms do not require any complex organizational, logistical, or training capacities to maintain and operate. Hence, they are usable by a large number of groups—the preferred kind of equipment of the armed forces of many poor countries and of guerrilla and other armed sub-state groups.[10]

- Many small weapons are so lightweight and can be assembled and reassembled with such ease that children as young as 10 years of age can use them. While the phenomenon of child soldiers is not a new one, the easy availability of lightweight arms in the contemporary era has boosted the ability of children to participate in armed conflicts.[11]

- Their light weight and small size make these arms easy to conceal and smuggle. They are readily available on a burgeoning black market, and therefore easy for guerrilla groups, criminal organizations, and other interested buyers to obtain.[12]

- Major weapons become obsolete relatively quickly and are in constant need of new spare parts and maintenance. By contrast, small arms are sturdy enough to have a long "life," making it possible for them to be circulated from one conflict to another. For example, an F-5 jet fighter requires an inventory of about 60,000 spare parts, but an AK-47 Kalashnikov has only 16 moving parts. Small arms of World War II vintage and some even of World War I vintage are still used in today's conflicts.[13]

As the primary tools of warfare, small weapons have been put to increasing use: the number of conflicts active in any given year worldwide rose steadily from 1945 to 1992. According to the Wars, Armaments, and Development Research Unit at the University of Hamburg, that number peaked at 51 in 1992. Only with the resolution of several long-standing wars in Central America and southern Africa was the trend reversed. The number of armed conflicts declined to 37 in 1995. (See Figure 1.)[14]

According to a detailed analysis by researchers at the University of Uppsala in Sweden, only 6 out of 101 conflicts in the period 1989–96 were international, involving the forces or territory of more than one state. The 101 armed conflicts had as many as 254 separate conflict parties. The combatants typically are not only uniformed soldiers, but also guerrilla groups of various stripes, paramilitary forces, drug and organized crime bands, warlords, and vigilante hit squads. An estimated quarter of a million children are soldiers, and children under 18 years of age were among the combatants in 33 current or recent conflicts. Child combatants under 15 years of age fought in 26 of these conflicts. Project Ploughshares, a Canadian research group, reports that children participated in fighting in more than 80 percent of the countries at war in 1995.[15]

While the number of armed conflicts is still at a high level, few of them are high-intensity wars. Rather, most are what the Uppsala researchers call "minor" and "intermediate" armed conflicts—those that kill fewer than 1,000 persons in a single year. Examples include the violence in Northern Ireland, fighting between the Burmese govern-

Number of Armed Conflicts, 1946–95

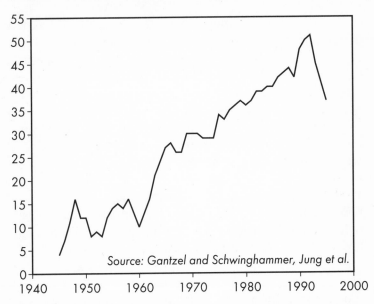

Source: Gantzel and Schwinghammer, Jung et al.

ment and several opposition groups, and armed clashes in Chad. But such violence disrupts societies in many ways. Both low- and high-intensity warfare continues to kill large numbers of people. During the first half of the 1990s, at least 3.2 million people died of war-related causes, bringing the cumulative toll since 1945 to at least 25 million. (See Figure 2.) This is probably a conservative figure. Civilians have accounted for a large share of the victims: perhaps 70 percent of all war casualties since World War II, but more than 90 percent in the 1990s.[16]

Many other countries experience near-war, what Dan Smith, director of the International Peace Research Institute in Oslo, describes as "widespread and even endemic" political violence "without quite meriting the name war." And societies that have emerged from long years of conflict often still experience considerable levels of political, intercommunal, or criminal violence. Though formally at peace now,

South Africa and El Salvador, for instance, have in recent years endured slayings that rival in number the people killed in earlier fighting.[17]

Such near-war violence may stem from a broad variety of causal factors, but it is sustained primarily by one: the easy availability of large amounts of weapons, especially small weapons. Michael Klare, director of the Five College Program in Peace and World Security Studies in Amherst, Massachusetts, argues that "the abundance of arms *at every level of society* means that any increase in inter-communal tensions and hostility will entail an increased likelihood of armed violence and bloodshed." For instance, in a single raid, 31 people, including eight children, were killed in late 1997 in clashes between rival cattle owners in northwestern Kenya. The influx of automatic weapons from war zones in neighboring Sudan and Somalia has transformed formerly low-key skirmishes into major violence.[18]

The dispersal of arms to private armies and militias, insurgent groups, criminal organizations, and other non-state actors feeds a cycle of violence at work in many societies that in turn causes even greater demand for guns. A variety of motivations spawn different kinds of violence, including *political* violence—pitting governments against insurgent forces fighting to overthrow the government or to achieve a separate state; *communal* violence—involving different ethnic, religious, or other identity-based groups; and *criminal* violence—involving drug traffickers, organized crime groups, or petty individual crime. And ordinary citizens in many countries are increasingly arming themselves in self-defense against widespread crime and violence.

South Africa and several Central American countries, among others, experienced a seamless transition from politically motivated to criminal violence in the early 1990s. Just beginning to recover from years of fighting, these and other countries now face conditions conducive to crime: severe economic and social inequalities, endemic poverty, a pervasive lack of jobs, and a culture of violence. Recently demobilized soldiers and former guerrilla fighters in particular

FIGURE 2

Deaths in Armed Conflicts, by 5-Year Period, 1946–95

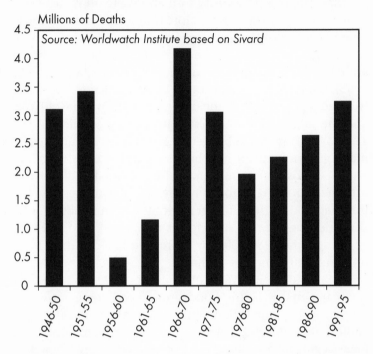

Millions of Deaths

Source: Worldwatch Institute based on Sivard

find themselves often poorly equipped to make a living in the civilian world; not surprisingly, many tend to fall back on the tools and skills they acquired during years of conflict, leading to increasing banditry in several countries. And weak or corrupt judiciary systems and ineffective police forces have given rise to vigilante squads intent on what they call "social cleansing"—killing individuals suspected of crimes or otherwise perceived as unwanted. The pervasive reliance on violence threatens the consolidation of still-weak democracies in several countries and compromises the reconstruction and social and economic development that war-torn societies need to get back on their feet.[19]

These factors feed what Michael Klare calls the privatization of security and violence—"a growing tendency of individuals, groups, and organizations to rely on private security forces rather than on the state's police and paramilitary formations."[20]

Indeed, private security formations are on the rise and civilian police are becoming more militarized just as national armies are shrinking in size. After climbing to a peak of 28.7 million persons in the world's regular, uniformed armed forces in 1988, the number declined to 23 million in 1995, or by about 20 percent. A range of factors have contributed to this decline, including the end of the Cold War and the termination of several long-lasting conflicts in the Third World, as well as budgetary difficulties encountered by many governments. It may be assumed that the strength of armed opposition groups has also declined, but reliable information is hard to come by. Data compiled by the International Institute for Strategic Studies in London for 27 countries suggest that such forces number at least 410,000, and might tally 500,000 or more if other countries with ongoing civil wars were included.[21]

Without Cold War-motivated sponsorship propping them up, many Third World armies and some insurgent forces can no longer be maintained at their previous size. Some armed forces are national armies in name only and have begun to fragment. Tales of soldiers going unpaid or underpaid for months on end abound. In consequence, large numbers of them turn to commercial ventures to supplement their incomes, or resort to looting and extortion, to petty crime, even to mercenary activity.[22]

Private security forces come in several stripes. Some work for corporations; British Petroleum made headlines, for instance, when it announced that it had engaged a battalion of local soldiers to protect its oil-production facilities in Colombia against guerrilla attacks. Others, however, are contracting to carry out the tasks that national armies seem unable to accomplish: in recent years, several struggling governments—including those of Sierra Leone, Angola, Zaire, and Papua New Guinea—have hired private mercenaries to help fight insurgent groups. But the most important phenomenon—in terms of the number of people involved—seems to be those private security services that, in some ways at least, closely resemble police forces.[23]

In several countries, private security forces rival or outstrip the size of the public police, and in some—among them Australia, South Africa, and the United States—even the national army. (See Table 1.) In the United States, there are now roughly three times as many private security guards as there are police officers. Only 280,000 in 1950, they were estimated at about 1.5 million in 1990; industry executives expect the number of private guards to surge to 2 million by the year 2000, although some experts say that level may already have been reached. While the number of private security personnel that are armed (legally or illegally) is uncertain, one report contends that today gun-toting private guards "have more firepower than the combined police

TABLE 1

Private Security, Public Police, and Military Forces, Selected Countries, Late 1980s, Early 1990s

Country	Private Security Forces[1]	Public Police Forces[2]	Military Armed Forces[3]	All Forces, Relative to Population
	(thousands)			(per 1,000)
United States	1,500	600	1,620	14
Britain	250[4]	190	233	11
South Africa	180	146	100	10
Colombia	100	na	146	7
France	96	110	504	12
Australia	90[4]	47	58	11
Israel	40	15	185	41
Spain	25[5]	119	210	9
Netherlands	13[6]	38	67	8
Belgium	7	15	47	7
New Zealand	5	na	10	4
Finland	3	12	32	9

[1]Data for late 1980s. [2]Data for late 1980s and 1990. [3]Data for 1995. [4]High end of range of estimates. [5]Includes personnel of registered companies only. [6]Could reach 30,000 according to government estimates
Sources: See endnote 24.

forces of the nation's 30 largest urban centers." At the same time, however, hundreds of millions of dollars' worth of surplus military equipment is being transferred to local police. Some 80 percent of U.S. cities have paramilitary police units that often train with elite military forces and apply military tactics to their work.[24]

As concern about crime and violence grows, individuals, groups, and businesses continue to invest growing amounts of money in private security ventures. In Latin America, public and private security expenses consume 13-15 percent of the region's combined gross domestic product—surpassing these countries' welfare expenditures. In 1990, annual spending for private security in the United States reached $52 billion, compared with a $30 billion budget for the country's police forces. Fifty-two billion dollars is more than any country other than the United States spends on its military. By the year 2000, U.S. expenditures on private law enforcement may reach $100 billion.[25]

If the trend toward private security forces is beneficial, this is true only for some—not necessarily those in need of security services, but rather those who have the ability to pay. Indeed, from Brazil to Pakistan to the United States, there is a rise of walled-in and guarded exclusive communities housing the better-off in society. This is happening at the same time that rising overall security-related spending siphons off scarce resources from programs that, by enhancing human wellbeing and strengthening the social fabric, help reduce the incidence of crime.[26]

As Easy As Buying Fish in the Market

In El Salvador, hand grenades "are commonly carried by
many citizens in their pockets and on their belts, and
increasingly are used to settle personal arguments."
—*Edward Laurance, Monterey Institute of
International Studies, California, 1996.*[27]

Small arms are so ubiquitous that many regions of the
world find themselves awash in them. A recent remark by
a local political leader in the Philippines captures the situation in many nations: firearms are so easily available, he
said, that acquiring them is "as easy as buying fish in the
market." Reliable data are very hard to obtain. Nevertheless,
the numbers that are available are staggering.[28]

One analyst put the number of firearms in worldwide
circulation at 500 million. This surely must be a conservative
estimate. Given the pervasive lack of information, even *Jane's
Infantry Weapons*—probably the most authoritative source on
small arms—offers no more than a listing of the kinds of pistols, rifles, sub-machine guns, machine guns, mortars, and
anti-tank weapons that are thought to be in service with
national armies around the world. There is little interest on
the part of governments in collecting such data, which of
course handicaps efforts to devise effective policies for small-
arms control.[29]

Some rough quantitative data exist for military rifles.
The most notorious assault rifle is the AK-47, also known by
its inventor's name, Kalashnikov. Manufactured in the former Soviet Union and in nine other countries, more than 70
million Kalashnikovs have been produced in some 100 different versions since 1947; most of these are still in use by
the armies of 78 countries and countless guerrilla groups the
world over. In Mozambique, one of the countries with the
largest number of these rifles, an AK-47 is emblazoned on
the national flag. According to the Bonn International
Center for Conversion (BICC), the standard black-market
price for an AK-47 is about $200, but it is far lower in areas

where the rifle is abundant. A United Nations (U.N.) report says that in Uganda an AK-47 can be purchased for the price of a chicken, and in northern Kenya, for the price of a goat.[30]

Still, this symbol of massive, if low-tech, violence shares its claim to fame with some other assault rifles that are in use by a large number of national armed forces. Among them are the U.S.-made M-16, of which 8 million copies have been turned out, the German G-3 (7 million), the Belgian-designed FN-FAL (5 to 7 million), and the Israeli Uzi machine pistol (10 million). In addition to licensed production of these and other small weapons, several countries are apparently flooding the world market with counterfeit (unauthorized) versions. All in all, more than 100 million military-style rifles are thought to exist worldwide.[31]

Beyond the small arms found in military arsenals there is of course a very large number of "civilian" firearms. These are generally weapons with less firepower or less-rapid firing capacity. But the military-civilian dividing line is not always clear. First, some civilian firearms can be converted to automatic or semi-automatic weapons (hence more closely resembling military-style arms). Second, an unknown number of assault rifles and other military-style weapons are in the possession of civilians, though often illegally.

No one really knows how many weapons are in circulation among the general population of most countries. The first international effort to gain some insight into the problem was a recent study by the U.N. Commission on Crime Prevention and Criminal Justice. It conducted a survey of member states to collect and compare data on the manufacturing, trade, and private possession of firearms, on national regulations of firearms, and on homicides, suicides, and accidents involving firearms. Forty-six nations, with 68 percent of the world's population, responded, although some provided only part of the information requested.[32]

The survey shows just how far the world community is from having even a rough idea of the order of magnitude of private firearms ownership. The combined official figure of 34 million firearms in private possession for the 35 countries that provided data probably represents little more than the tip of the arsenal iceberg. Russia, for instance, reported a figure of 3.6 million, but is generally thought to have a huge number of illegal guns in circulation, with the black market being fed by profuse leaks from the military's arsenal. In Canada, to take another example, the number of legitimate owners is unknown; instead of the 7 million figure submitted to the U.N., some think there may be as many as 21–25 million firearms in private possession. In addition to the problem of illegal possession, the U.N. survey has another obvious gap—not only did some important countries (such as China, for instance) not participate, but even some of the participating countries (such as the United States) provided only partial information. Only if most countries conduct a detailed domestic arms census will it be possible to shed more light on the situation.[33]

The United States is without doubt one of the countries with the largest private firearms arsenals, and very likely the leading one worldwide. There are a quarter of a million federally licensed firearms dealers in the country—20 times the number of McDonald's restaurants. Estimates of private firearm ownership in the United States run from 192 million in a recent Justice Department study, to 230 million according to the U.S. National Rifle Association, to a figure of 250 million put forward by the Federal Bureau of Investigation (FBI). At the high end of that range, this would mean one firearm for every American, from infant to senior citizen. Aside from illegal transactions, legitimate domestic production adds some 3-6 million firearms annually to the stockpile, and imports up to another 1 million. (See Figure 3.) But about half a million firearms are reported stolen in non-commercial thefts alone each year. The United States is now the only industrialized country in the world that allows

> **There are a quarter of a million federally licensed firearms dealers in the United States—20 times the number of McDonald's restaurants.**

its citizens to own military-style assault rifles—weapons that account for an estimated 1 percent of all U.S. firearms but, according to the Urban Institute, for at least 8 percent of gun-related crimes.[34]

Although high levels of gun ownership do not automatically translate into rampant violence, the easy availability of guns does make a difference, particularly in societies where significant economic inequality holds forth, where poverty and unemployment lead people to commit crimes as a survival tactic, where the social fabric is under severe strain, where strong ethnic or class animosities persist, and where the legitimacy of political institutions is being questioned.

According to the U.N. survey, Brazil has by far the highest number of firearm homicides—41,000 per year—and places a close second to South Africa in the rate of killings per total population. The murder rate in São Paulo has reached one per hour, and 90 percent of all killings are committed with firearms. There are an estimated 18.5 million firearms in the country, only one third of which are registered. In Brazil as elsewhere, as the general level of violence goes up, so does the number of citizens that carry personal guns, and confidence in the police's ability to provide public safety declines. Behind the large-scale violence in Brazil are serious social problems, including high unemployment, drug trafficking, and a spate of vigilante justice.[35]

The difficult economic and political transition in Russia has spawned rising crime and mafia-like organizations that stage spectacular gangland-style killings to eliminate business rivals—there were almost 1,000 contract murders in 1996 alone. The resulting sense of insecurity, in turn, has encouraged ordinary citizens to arm themselves; 14 percent of Russians daily carry weapons for self-defense. Ownership of—mostly illegal—arms in Russia is exploding. The burgeoning black market is apparently being fed by a constant stream of assault rifles, sub-machine guns, pistols, grenades, and explosives from military depots even though the private ownership of military-style weapons is illegal.[36]

FIGURE 3

U.S. Firearms Production, 1946–95

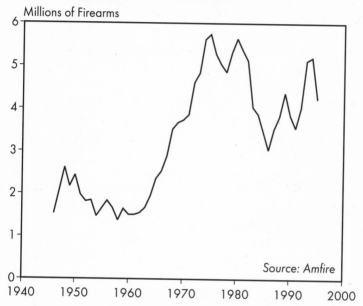

Millions of Firearms

Source: Amfire

Although the United States is far more stable than Russia, there also, high levels of gun ownership and a laissez-faire attitude toward guns translate into broad-scale violence. More people are killed with guns in a typical week than in all of Western Europe in a whole year. And there are more U.S. firearm homicides in a single day than in a year in Japan. A recent study by the Centers for Disease Control and Prevention says that U.S. adolescents are 12 times more likely to be killed by gunfire than youngsters in all other industrialized countries.[37]

The danger that easy availability of weapons may translate into impulsive recourse to violence is probably greatest in societies that are struggling to rebuild themselves after long years of warfare and to shake off the legacy of a culture of violence. They face the particular challenge of reintegrating large numbers of former soldiers or guerrillas into civilian life, in a situation where warfare has destroyed a large portion of their public infrastructure, economic activity remains handicapped, national treasuries are depleted, and foreign lenders are demanding belt-tightening. Though political violence may finally be absent, social and criminal violence is often ascendant. That kind of violence may in turn provoke countermeasures that could well rekindle political confrontations. Peace, so difficult to attain in the first place, rests on a shaky foundation.

Among the regions that are of particular concern are Central America and southern Africa. Emerging from its devastating civil war of the 1980s, El Salvador has been formally at peace since 1992. Yet the number of violent deaths since that year—some 20,000—comes close, on an annual basis, to rivaling the number of people killed during the war—about 75,000 over a period of 13 years. The postwar violence stems from several factors.[38]

The large majority of 40,000 demobilized soldiers and guerrillas have been unable to establish themselves in civilian society. Some of them have taken up arms left over from the war. Formed by former soldiers and by disoriented youth, heavily armed Salvadoran criminal groups are responsible for murders, kidnappings, and robberies throughout the country. Gang members are buying and smuggling weapons left over from the civil war into neighboring countries and the United States, and there is evidence that some of them have formed alliances with Mexican and Colombian drug traffickers.[39]

With unemployment running at an estimated 50 percent and roughly two thirds of the Salvadoran population living in extreme poverty, crime is rampant. "Military weapons and poverty are proving to be a deadly combination," comments Edward Laurance. Furthermore, because of corruption and an ineffective judicial system, vigilante justice has been on the rise; new death squads have emerged that target people considered to be criminals or "anti-social elements." In reaction to rising crime and violence, ordinary citizens are arming themselves as well.[40]

Southern Africa confronts similar challenges. On the

order of 9 million small arms are thought to be in the arsenals of the armies of South Africa, Angola, Mozambique, and Zimbabwe, but substantial additional numbers of weapons are in private hands, in hidden caches, or flowing in secret arms-trading channels that cross borders with impunity. Although no one knows for sure just how many firearms are in circulation, there is no doubt that the region is flooded with weapons. The 3 to 4 million firearms that are licensed to private citizens in South Africa, for example, represent little more than a fraction of the total. Decades of warfare and violent political struggle have given rise to a pervasive gun culture. "Light weapons have become a form of currency throughout the region," writes Jacklyn Cock of the University of Witwatersrand.[41]

In the United States, more people are killed with guns in a typical week than in all of Western Europe in a whole year.

Substantial numbers of people in the region, including former combatants, rely on criminal activities to make a living. Soaring crime rates, in turn, are generating demand for yet more arms for self-protection and are propelling private security services to greater prominence. Under these circumstances, prospects for peace and development are clouded, as Cock explains: "In South Africa the level of violent crime linked to this proliferation threatens the consolidation of democracy. In Mozambique, northern Namibia, and Angola the proliferation of light weapons, especially anti-personnel landmines, threatens to subvert social and economic reconstruction."[42]

In South Africa, the political violence of the years of transition away from Apartheid (1990–93), during which some 10,000 people were killed, has declined dramatically. But according to Cock, there has been a parallel, equally dramatic increase in criminal violence fueled by high unemployment and economic hardship. Military-style weapons such as the AK-47 and the G-3 are increasingly used in rob-

beries and in the so-called "taxi wars"—clashes between
competing taxi owners who have employed hitmen to kill
passengers and drivers of their rivals. In a sense, South Africa
is being hit by an arms boomerang: the instability that
South Africa's Apartheid regime sowed in Mozambique by
supporting the ruthless RENAMO rebels and supplying them
with weapons is now hitting home. Many of these weapons
are being smuggled back into South Africa, joining other
arms flowing in from Namibia and Angola and those "leaking" from weapons depots inside South Africa.[43]

A top official of the Mozambique Defense Force, Lazaro
Mathe, has said that Mozambique, with a population of 15
million, has more weapons than people. Others have estimated the number at 10 million. The number of AK-47s
alone is at least 1.5 million, and perhaps as large as 6 million. During the country's civil war, the government and the
rebels were supplied with large amounts of small weapons
by South Africa and the Soviet Union. The antagonists, in
turn, "passed out weapons almost indiscriminately, arming
not just soldiers but everyone they could find," as Suzanne
Daley, a reporter for the *New York Times* put it. It is widely
believed that weapons collection by a U.N. peacekeeping
force was limited and ultimately ineffectual because combatants retained their best weapons and there was no
attempt to collect weapons held by civilians. Now, poorly
paid soldiers and police officers are selling weapons—the
one commodity that seems boundless—to what appears to
be an insatiable market in South Africa.[44]

The Mozambican experience seems likely to repeat
itself in Angola, another of the countries that Apartheid-era
South Africa sought to destabilize and one that has been at
war from 1975 to 1994. Perhaps as many as 90 percent of
Angolans privately possess firearms. The government's campaign to recover arms from civilians—as required under the
country's peace accord—has so far made little more than a
small dent.[45]

The picture that emerges globally is one where individual countries and entire regions are inundated with both

military-style small weapons and civilian firearms. Current controls—to the extent they exist at all—appear hopelessly inadequate for dealing with the, so far, unencumbered flow of arms. Many countries are just beginning to recognize the potential for large-scale violence and instability that this massive availability of firepower implies.

Lethal Harvests

What crop costs a hundred times more to reap than to plant and has no market value when harvested?
—*Tony Cunningham, European Parliament, 1995.*[46]

The AK-47 rifle is one of the key symbols of light weapons proliferation. But even more numerous is the anti-personnel landmine. This is a weapon that stands out in a particularly cruel way: it continues to kill long after a conflict has come to an end; it cannot distinguish between soldiers and civilians or between adults and children; it is turning huge numbers of people into hapless victims; and it can inhibit the rehabilitation of war-torn countries by impeding agriculture and the movement of people and goods.

Thanks to an insistent campaign by hundreds of non-governmental organizations (NGOs) around the globe that are working to ban landmines, a great deal of information has been gathered in recent years, helping to raise awareness. More than 250 million landmines have been produced since the early 1970s: approximately 60 million anti-tank mines and 190 million anti-personnel mines (the following discussion is concerned only with the latter kind). Production may run as high as 10 to 30 million each year, allowing continued heavy use and stockpiling. Some 100 companies in 50 countries have been producing more than 360 different types of mines. At least 35 countries have exported mines in a trade worth about $100 million per year.[47]

An estimated 120 million anti-personnel landmines are

TABLE 2

Estimated Number of Uncleared Landmines, Most Affected Countries, Relative to Population and Territory, 1997[1]

Country	Number of Mines (millions)	Mines per 1,000 Inhab.	Mines per Square Km	Amputees per 1,000 Inhab.
Egypt	23	361	23	na
Iran	16	254	10	na
Angola	15	1,304	12	3.0
Cambodia	10	917	55	2.6
Iraq	10	467	23	1.0
Afghanistan	10	465	15	1.6
China	10	8	1	na
Bosnia	6[2]	1,667	118	na
Croatia	3	682	52	na
Mozambique	3	182	5	0.4
Somalia	1	105	2	na
Eritrea	1	278	11	0.6
Sudan	1	35	0.4	0.2

[1]The per 1,000 inhabitants and per square kilometer data are averages that in some cases understate the severity of mine infestation in parts of a country. For instance, as many as 90 percent of the mines in Iraq may be located in the Kurdish region. [2]High end of range of estimates.

Sources: See endnote 48.

currently scattered in 71 countries, most of them poor developing countries. In some of the worst-affected nations, the number of mines rivals or surpasses the number of people. (See Table 2.) Because mines can remain deadly for decades and capacities to get rid of them are severely limited, many countries will suffer for generations. In fact, mines continue to be laid far faster than they are being removed: in an average year, clearing operations worldwide struggle to retrieve roughly 100,000 mines, even as an estimated 2 million—some say 5 million—additional mines are being laid.[48]

A growing number of analysts are now questioning the military utility of landmines. Indeed, scattered indiscriminately, landmines are not so much weapons of war as instruments of terror. They leave a legacy of individual death and suffering, debilitating burdens on public health sectors, and socio-economic decay. Of approximately 1 million persons who have been killed or maimed by landmines since 1975, some 80 percent were civilians. Today, mines kill roughly 9,600 people worldwide each year and maim another 14,400—every 20 minutes or so, a person steps on a mine. Even though this is double the number of victims recorded in 1980, it is a conservative estimate. In Cambodia, one of the worst-affected countries, one out of 234 persons is an amputee.[49]

Mine blasts cause horrific wounds and typically require multiple surgery. On average, a surviving victim is estimated to incur lifetime costs of $3,000 to $5,000 for surgery and prosthetic devices. But expenses can go far higher if adequate care is available; some Western relief workers who have become mine victims have run up medical bills in the hundreds of thousands of dollars. About one third of all surviving victims require amputations; at present, there are 250,000 amputees from mine accidents. Coping with the disproportionate health care needs of mine-blast survivors can easily overwhelm not only their family's resources, but also their country's health and social systems. The World Health Organization concluded that no more than 15-20 percent of rehabilitation needs are currently being met.[50]

Scattered randomly, landmines have become a ubiquitous threat to the normal functioning of many societies, long after the last shots of a war have been fired. Without effective demining programs, large areas of land remain inaccessible, refugees are discouraged from returning home, peasants cannot work their fields because they have been mined or cannot transport their produce to markets because roads are mined, economic activity in affected areas grinds to a halt, and reconstruction is hindered. The economies of the countries most infested with landmines tend to be agrarian and relatively weak, particularly after long years of crippling warfare. Hence, they are ill-equipped to cope with the landmine crisis.

In the Vietnamese province of Quang Tri, 22 years after

the end of the war, 3,000–4,000 hectares of farmland, enough to feed 35,000 people, still cannot be cultivated because of mines and unexploded ordinance. In different parts of Afghanistan, agricultural production could be increased by 88 to 200 percent in the absence of landmines; in Cambodia, it could be raised by 135 percent. In Libya, 27 percent of arable land is unusable, due to World War II minefields. In northern Iraq, some 17 percent of arable land is mine infested, a portion rising to 50 percent along border areas. Edward Laurance writes that the presence of landmines has cut the amount of land available for agriculture in the worst-affected countries in half.[51]

Experience suggests that it takes 100 times as long to detect, remove, and disarm a mine as to plant it. A mine is extremely cheap to manufacture (typically $3–$20), but expensive to remove ($300–$1,000). The estimated costs of clearing all mines worldwide are astronomical, ranging from $33 to $85 billion, while demining efforts around the world, funded to the tune of about $100 million annually, remain severely underfinanced. And while mine technology continues to evolve, making mines harder to detect and defuse, clearance techniques are essentially 1940s vintage. Thus demining is extremely dangerous. Accidents happen at a rate of one per 1,000-2,000 mines lifted.[52]

Even if the proliferation of landmines stopped overnight, with the present global demining capacity it would take almost 1,100 years to get rid of all those mines already scattered. But because the challenge is a growing one, the scope of clearance efforts would have to be increased more than 20-fold just to prevent the problem from getting worse.[53]

Feeding the Habit

That small weapons are so ubiquitous should not come as a surprise: a multitude of seemingly inexhaustible sources feed the market. Some of the weapons produced each year never cross any borders, being destined for domestic recipients. But international transfers play a crucial role. These run the gamut from direct government-to-government sales and government-approved exports by private arms manufacturers; to covert deliveries by government agencies and a variety of black market deals involving private arms merchants; to capture of arms by insurgent forces or theft from government arsenals; to, finally, the often illicit passing of weapons from one area of conflict to another.

Governments may decry the latter kinds of deals, but government-sanctioned sales are by far the most important source of arms proliferation. Officials in Washington and Moscow like to think that the Cold War period is history now; but the extensive arms transfers carried out by the two superpowers during those decades continue to have a deadly impact.

Whereas the ability to manufacture major weapons is limited to a fairly small number of advanced industrial countries, the capacity to produce small arms is far more widespread. In part, this is because smaller weapons tend to be less technically challenging, but it also stems from the spread of licensed production and the frequent practice of reverse-engineering. Countries like Russia, China, and the United States, along with several European nations, are major producers of small arms. But the United Nations Institute for Disarmament Research (UNIDIR) in Geneva has identified close to 300 companies in 52 countries that were manufacturing small arms and related equipment in 1994—a 25 percent increase in the number of such countries since the mid-1980s. Licensed production is taking place in at least 22 developing countries, 16 of which are also exporting these kinds of weapons. In addition, insurgent and opposition groups in several nations possess the capability to produce simple small-caliber weapons. Among them are the Irish Republican Army, the Palestine Liberation Organization, and groups in Mexico, India, Pakistan, and some African countries. The largely lawless Northwest Frontier Province of Pakistan, for instance, is home to a large number of gun workshops. Although no statistics are available, it would appear that worldwide production of small arms easily runs to several million, if not tens of millions, of units each year.[54]

Most international transfers take place in the form of either direct government-to-government transfers (vast quantities were provided by the two superpowers during the Cold War, either at heavily discounted prices or for free) or commercial sales involving private companies (the most important source of transfers since the end of the Cold War). Unfortunately, available statistics for such transactions do not distinguish between major and small arms. Michael Klare estimates that of $25.9 billion worth of arms that U.S. firms were authorized to export in 1989–93, small arms accounted for perhaps a third—$8.6 billion worth. He reckons that anywhere from 10 to 20 percent of U.S. grant transfers of arms and ammunition (worth $55.2 billion in 1950–94) involved small arms.[55]

While too little information is available even about these official, "legal" sales authorized and acknowledged by governments, there are a multitude of secret and illegal deals by governments and others about which, due to their very nature, next to nothing is known. Most of the discussion revolves around anecdotal or circumstantial evidence. Still, transactions such as black-market sales, arms-for-natural resources barter, smuggling of stolen arms, and unauthorized transfers from original to secondary recipients appear to be much more significant with regard to light weapons than major weapon sales.[56]

Key among such transfers are covert arms deliveries by governments to insurgent and separatist groups in other countries. During the Cold War, this was a frequent tool of the United States and the Soviet Union, and helped spread massive amounts of weaponry that continues to fuel violent conflict and bedevil peacemaking efforts in many locales around the globe, particularly in Central America, southern Africa, and South Asia. Although less important to Washington and Moscow now, covert supplies are a practice that other governments have resorted to as well. For instance, Pakistan is delivering arms to Kashmiri insurgents, and Iran is supplying Kurdish rebels in Turkey.[57]

In addition to clandestine supplies by government agencies, the international black market is being fed by legions of private arms merchants and criminal organizations. According to Klare, black market sales have greatly expanded in recent years. Among some of the most important known recipients are Colombian drug cartels and the rival factions in Bosnia. Klare writes that "weak gun control laws and inadequate law enforcement have made the United States one of Latin America's main sources of black-market arms." The Mexican government is expressing growing alarm at the torrent of illegal U.S. firearms—thousands, if not tens of thousands, of firearms per year—that is flowing to drug cartels and guerrilla groups, and fueling a crime wave in Mexican cities.[58]

Often, black-market deals involve the barter of weapons for natural resources, animal products, drugs, and other commodities, or at least the financing of arms purchases through the sale of such commodities. (See Table 3.) R.T. Naylor, an economics professor at McGill University in Montreal, observes that "much of the world's contraband traffic in diamonds, precious gems, jade, ivory, teakwood, and 'recreational drugs', along with part of the traffic in looted antiquities, is either controlled at the source by an insurgent group or at least taxed by them. Thus, just as the growth of the international underground economy greatly facilitates the physical process of arms supply, simultaneously it makes it easier for insurgent groups to find the means to pay for them ..."[59]

Other important sources of weapons flows are the capture of arms by insurgent forces, the looting of military

TABLE 3

Selected Examples of Commodities-for-Arms Transactions, 1980s–90s

Country/ Region	Observation
Liberia, Sierra Leone	Charles Taylor and other Liberian warlords were trading timber, iron ore, and agricultural products for small arms and military training since 1990; Taylor earned up to $100 million a year.[1] In the early 1990s, government and rebel soldiers in neighboring Sierra Leone plundered diamond mines. Rebels exchanged diamonds for rocket launchers and Kalashnikovs from Taylor's forces.
Rwanda	In 1992, Egypt accepted future Rwandan tea harvests as collateral for $6 million worth of artillery, mortars, land mines, and assault rifles sent to the government; Egypt took delivery of $1 million in Rwandan tea before fighting in Rwanda's civil war damaged the tea bushes.
Southern Africa	Many ivory and rhino horn poachers in Zimbabwe and Mozambique are ex-soldiers involved in both buying and selling small arms on the black market. UNITA rebel forces in Angola earn $450-500 million a year in diamond sales. Also, UNITA paid for South African military support with ivory, slaughtering tens of thousands of elephants. RENAMO rebels in Mozambique bartered game (meat, hides, ivory) for guns.
Cambodia	Khmer Rouge are financing their military effort by trading timber and gems to "renegades" in the Thai military who control the Cambodian-Thai border, earning $100-250 million a year. Other Cambodian factions also finance their armies with timber sales.
China	Pingyuan in Yunnan province is a major drug and arms trafficking center. Most of the weapons used in criminal activities in 24 of China's 31 provinces come in via Pingyuan from Burma and Vietnam.
Central America, Mexico	Black market arms sales are linked to the illicit drug trade. Traffickers of guns and drugs often combine their operations and use the same routes and transportation systems.

[1]For comparative purposes, $100 million might purchase up to 400,000 assault rifles at typical, discounted prices.
Sources: See endnote 59.

depots, and leaks from government arsenals (that is, the theft and selloff of weapons by soldiers). The seizure of weapons from government armies has long been essential to Latin American guerrilla forces' acquisition of arms. But in recent years, it has also proven important for the embryonic armies of Croatia, Slovenia, Bosnia, and Georgia, for example, and for armed opposition groups in places as different as Algeria, Sierra Leone, and Cambodia. In Somalia, following the army's disintegration at the peak of the civil war in early 1992, some 500,000 weapons ended up in the hands of competing warlords. In South Africa, large quantities of small arms stolen from military bases and armories by white right-wing organizations or supplied to them by sympathetic police forces, along with leaks of weapons from guerrilla armies' depots, fueled the political violence that gripped the country in the first half of the 1990s.[60]

One of the most spectacular recent examples of depot looting occurred in Albania. Triggered by the collapse of fraudulent investment schemes that cost many citizens their entire savings, large numbers of Albanians revolted against the economic and political conditions in their country; most police and military depots were ransacked. The number of weapons seized has variously been estimated at 500,000 to 800,000, and the Defense Ministry reported that a staggering 10.5 billion bullets had been stolen. Within a few weeks, virtually everyone in this country of 3.5 million people was armed, including women and children. The Defense Ministry became so desperate that, under provisions of the state of emergency proclaimed in March 1997, it warned it would lay landmines around its ammunition depots in order to prevent them from being looted. Though the situation in Albania is calmer now, it remains unstable. Armed gangs still terrorize large areas of the country. And some of the seized weapons may have been sold to Albanians in neighboring Macedonia and in the Kosovo area of Serbia—territories where tensions run high—and to Greece.[61]

A different leakage problem is found in Russia. Researchers Ksenia Gonchar and Peter Lock cite a a long list of factors that facilitate the rise of illicit arms production and trade. Among them are weak authority and oversight of the government over the arms industry and the armed forces, weak law enforcement and porous borders, and general social disorder. In addition, the desperate state of affairs in the armed forces (discussed in more detail later) virtually invites soldiers to sell off portions of the immense arsenal accumulated during Soviet times. Michael Klare notes that parts of the armed forces "are reported to be selling some of their excess weapons to foreign buyers and to combatants in the various internal conflicts now underway in the ex-Soviet republics." During the Chechen war, for instance, poorly equipped and starving Russian soldiers were trading their Kalashnikovs for food. "The Chechens bought all their supplies and weapons from us; otherwise," one conscript explained, "we wouldn't have had money to eat."[62]

Unstable countries are not the only places where thefts from military arsenals occur. In China, for instance, where the central government retains far more authority than its Russian counterpart, criminal gangs apparently have little trouble gaining access to weaponry, due to inadequate controls in the arms industry, the army, and the police force. Even in the United States, a General Accounting Office report found in 1993 that small arms parts (including parts for the M-16 military rifle) are being systematically stolen from the Pentagon's repair shops and warehouses, and then sold to gun dealers.[63]

A source of growing importance for both legal and illegal arms sales are surplus stocks. Casting off excess weapons is not a new phenomenon: since the 1950s, the U.S. government has given away or sold cheaply almost 3 million military-style firearms. And this practice is of particular significance now that the end of the Cold War has left many countries of NATO and the former Warsaw Pact with far more military hardware than they need. Narrow cost-benefit considerations have led several governments to sell off surplus equipment, often at bargain rates, instead of dismantling or destroying it. Cheap secondhand arms are particularly attractive to buyers who cannot afford newly produced, state-of-the-art weaponry. Michael Brzoska and Herbert Wulf of the Bonn International Center for Conversion (BICC) in Germany point out that "what is surplus for a modern army is still useful for fighting enemies who are...armed with outdated weapons." Indeed, some of the surplus weapons transferred as far back as 40 years ago by the U.S. military are still in use today by the armed forces of countries in Latin America, Asia, and Africa.[64]

Researchers at BICC reckon that the current cumulative inventory of surplus major weapons systems worldwide runs to about 165,000 pieces—tanks, artillery, jet fighters, large naval ships—or about one out of three in the existing arsenals. Between 1990 and 1995, more than 18,000 of these were transferred, involving 41 exporting countries and 90 importers. Not only has the trade in surplus arms reached new records, BICC finds, but many governments scrutinize exports of these items far less than they do new weapons sales. Although there is a lack of reliable data for surplus small arms, anecdotal evidence suggests that the numbers are also substantial. For instance, Turkey received 304,000 formerly East German Kalashnikovs and 83 million rounds of ammunition from Germany.[65]

Since the 1950s, the U.S. government has given away or sold cheaply almost 3 million military-style firearms.

A different kind of surplus arms are those that get transferred—illicitly—from one hotspot of the world to another. Often, when a conflict in one country comes to an end, the weapons—particularly the small weapons—are sold or donated by former combatants to belligerents in other countries. Indeed, as Natalie Goldring of the British American Security Information Council, an NGO, points out, "because light weapons may last for decades, a single weapon may be transferred many ... times."[66]

The U.S. supply of arms to the Afghan Mujahideen during the 1980s provides one of the most striking examples of weapons flows from one recipient to another. In response to the 1979 Soviet invasion, millions of tons of military materiel—precise amounts are unknown due to secrecy and poor recordkeeping—were pumped into the region via Pakistan by the U.S. Central Intelligence Agency (CIA). Estimates of the value of the weapons (which included arms originally made in China, Turkey, Egypt, Britain, India, and the Soviet Union) run at $6-$9 billion.[67]

U.S.-supplied weapons sustained the resistance to the Soviet occupation, and later fueled a ferocious, ongoing civil war among competing Afghan factions after the Soviet withdrawal in 1989. But the arms "pipeline" had massive leaks from the very beginning and fed violence and instability in large portions of South and Central Asia. Afghan rebels and officers of the Pakistani ISI (Inter-Services Intelligence) diverted large amounts of military equipment for resale, with the proceeds subsequently invested primarily in the drug trade. The Mujahideen fighters may have received as little as 30–40 percent of total deliveries intended for them. ISI supposedly had at some point stashed away 3 million Kalashnikov rifles that were siphoned off the pipeline.[68]

Weapons from the Afghan pipeline turned Pakistan's North West Frontier Province into a massive arms bazaar in which "virtually any type of small arm or light weapon [is] available for purchase," according to Chris Smith, Senior Research Fellow at the Centre for Defence Studies at King's College in London. "Ownership of an AK-47 is now *de rigeur*," he reports, and "land disputes now involve the use of mortars and rocket-propelled grenades." Weapons out of the Afghan pipeline have also aggravated violence in Pakistan's Sindh province and particularly its capital, Karachi, which is now a major nexus of drug and arms trafficking in South Asia. And they have been smuggled into civil-war-plagued Tajikistan, into India's Punjab region, to Muslims in northern India who feel increasingly threatened by Hindu extremists, and into Kashmir, where they increased the severity of the violence between Indian forces and pro-independence militants. Furthermore, there are reports of some of these weapons turning up in Sri Lanka, Burma, and Algeria.[69]

The sole type of weapon whose uncertain whereabouts seems to have elicited concern in Washington is the Stinger surface-to-air missile. This is a shoulder-fired weapon of which at least 900 units were delivered to the Mujahideen. Some 340 appear to have been used against Soviet forces. Some missiles were captured by the Afghan army and passed to the Soviets; but others allegedly ended up in the hands of either government or armed opposition groups of several far-flung places: Bosnia, Algeria, Lebanon, Qatar, Turkey, Iran, Pakistan, Chechnya, China, North Korea, Sri Lanka, and Tajikistan (some of these may have originated with rebel groups in Angola and Nicaragua who, like the Mujahideen, were supplied by the United States). Worried about a weapon able to shoot down military and civilian airplanes, the CIA made a frantic but largely unsuccessful effort to recover the Stingers, offering as much as $65 million for their return.[70]

The story of the leaky Afghanistan arms pipeline is far from an aberration. Weapons left behind by the United States in Vietnam in the 1970s showed up in the Middle East and Central America; U.S. armaments pumped into Central America in the 1980s are now part of a regional black market; weapons from Lebanon's civil war of the 1970s and 1980s have been shipped to Bosnia; and surplus arms from Mozambique's civil war are being smuggled by former rebel soldiers to bands of criminals in Zimbabwe and South Africa. (See Table 4.)[71]

Important regional secondhand arms markets have emerged in Bangkok, Beirut, Peshawar, and Prague. In these and other places, guerrilla and separatist forces, embargoed states, private militias, and criminal organizations are stocking up their arsenals.[72]

TABLE 4

Selected Examples of Arms Transfers from Hotspot to Hotspot, 1980s–90s

Initial Recipient	Subsequent Recipient(s)
Vietnam	Vietnam inherited 1.8 million U.S.-made small arms and close to 150,000 tons of ammunition following the withdrawal of U.S. troops in 1975. Much of this was acquired by Cuba, and then by the Sandinista government in Nicaragua and the FMLN rebels in El Salvador. Leftover U.S. arms also went to Chilean rebels.
Palestine Liberation Organization	The CIA obtained several tons of Soviet-made munitions that had been confiscated from PLO forces by the Israelis in 1982, and transferred them to the Nicaraguan Contras.
Nicaragua, El Salvador	Weapons remaining from civil wars of the 1980s are being shipped to new areas of conflict. Contra arms being sold to drug cartels and rebels in Colombia (via Panama). Some AK-47s and rocket-propelled grenades formerly held by the Contras and FMLN found their way to Zapatista rebels in Chiapas, Mexico. Some ex-FMLN guns went to Peru's MRTA rebels, and to Salvadoran gangs in the United States.
Ethiopia, Sudan, Somalia	The Mengistu government offered several thousand U.S.-made weapons inherited from the previous, pro-Western government to the FMLN rebels in El Salvador. Following the collapse of the Mengistu regime in Ethiopia, weapons flooded into Somalia. Surplus arms left over from recent conflicts in Sudan and Somalia flowed into Kenya, where they are used in deadly confrontations by rival cattle herders.
Mozambique, Angola	Large amounts of leftover weapons from conflicts in Mozambique and Angola (many of them originally supplied to rebel forces by South Africa's Apartheid regime) are being smuggled into South Africa, Namibia, Zimbabwe, and Zambia.

Sources: See endnote 71.

The Challenge of Shrinking Armies

The shrinkage of many armies around the world during the past decade is in principle a highly welcome development. Yet, it has brought with it some new challenges. Simply getting people out of their uniforms or battle fatigues is only the first step. If the next step—reintegrating ex-soldiers into civilian society—fails, rising crime, arms smuggling, violence, and instability are the likely consequences, as the experience of several countries suggests. Both the "surplus" soldiers and their weapons are of concern.

Since the mid-1980s, the largest cuts in absolute terms occurred in China, Iraq, Russia, Vietnam, and the United States. The U.S. armed forces are at their lowest level since 1950. (Demobilization does not necessarily mean unequivocal demilitarization: at least in some cases, the United States being a prominent example, manpower is being cut to save money for modern equipment purchases.) In relative terms, the developments in Argentina, El Salvador, Eritrea, Ethiopia, Liberia, Mozambique, Namibia, Nicaragua, and some other countries are also impressive. These states demobilized half or more of their armies. In addition, Angola, South Africa, and Guatemala are completing similarly large efforts. In most cases, demobilization is taking place as these countries finally emerge from long years of internal warfare. (See Table 5.)[73]

The demobilization experience has varied enormously in different countries around the world. Programs in the United States and Germany, for example, are relatively well funded and well managed, whereas the experience in the successor states of the former Soviet Union (FSU) and in many poor countries has been far less smooth. But this is not just a result of inadequate planning and management capabilities; it also reflects the state of the overall economy. The United States and Germany can offer considerable public services and safety nets.[74]

In some countries—principally those previously at

war—the process of demobilizing soldiers and subsequently reintegrating them into civilian society is proving to be an enormous challenge. Demobilization typically involves the temporary encampment of soldiers (or insurgent fighters) in areas where they can be disarmed, provided with food, medical care, and money, and given some basic training and orientation to help them master civilian life. But in poor countries, the overall financial resources available for demobilization are typically insufficient. For instance, encampment sites often lack proper sanitation, accommodations, and adequate supplies of food and water.[75]

Because of insufficient funds or due to political and bureaucratic obstacles, the demobilization process can at times be painfully slow, leading frustrated ex-combatants to riot or to desert (as happened in Mozambique and Angola, respectively). BICC concludes that "rapid visibility of the benefits of peace is ... required." Another issue of concern is the frequent lack of effective control over the weapons of soldiers waiting to be demobilized, including the question of secure storage of arms that have been collected during demobilization. Experience in several countries suggests that there is a danger that armaments may be stolen (and then sold to smugglers).[76]

Once former combatants have gone through the demobilization process, another, and perhaps even greater, challenge awaits them: reintegrating into civilian society. Apart from the possibility that ex-fighters may not be welcome in particular communities (in civil wars, the civilian population bear the brunt of the violence and are likely to resent those who tormented them), substantial numbers of soldiers do not possess any meaningful civilian work skills or experience; in fact, some, including the quarter million or so child soldiers worldwide, have known no life other than that in the military.[77]

"You cannot demobilize soldiers into nothing," as Thabo Mbeki, South Africa's deputy president, has commented. But finding a new livelihood—particularly in countries whose economies have been drained by long years of

TABLE 5

Demobilizations of Soldiers in Selected Developing Countries, Late 1980s and 1990s

Country	Number Demobilized (thousands)	Period	Soldiers Drawn from
Ethiopia	500	1991	Government
Cuba	120	Early 1990s	Government
Mozambique	90	1992-94	Government, rebels
Nicaragua	88	1992	Government, rebels
Argentina	83	1989-95	Government
Angola	70	1996-97	Government, rebels
Eritrea	48[1]	1991-94	Government
Namibia	43	1989	Government, rebels
South Africa	40	1995-99	Government, rebels
El Salvador	38	1992-93	Government, rebels
Liberia	33	1996-97	Warring militias
Uganda	32[2]	1992-94	Government
Chad	15	1992-94	Government
Guatemala	18[3]	1997	Government, rebels
Haiti	7[4]	1994	Government

[1] 12,000 demobilizations more planned. [2] 12,500 more planned. [3] In addition, some 180,000 members of a government paramilitary group (Civil Self-Defense Patrols) demobilized and disarmed. [4] Armed forces were abolished.

Sources: See endnote 73.

warfare—is an enormous challenge. Even where short-term jobs and benefits materialize, longer-term employment is far from assured. Many former combatants face tremendous difficulties because they have limited or inappropriate education and skills, and often little experience with the ways of the civilian world. Data on unemployment rates of ex-soldiers are scarce, but indications are that many struggle with prolonged unemployment or underemployment. Training in civilian skills is often either not available or inadequate. Jobs are scarce. As a result, the temptation to engage in banditry or other criminal activities as a means to survive may be hard to resist—particularly as it tends to be far more lucrative than eking out a precarious living as a subsistence farmer or day laborer. Others may decide to sell off weapons they retained to supplement otherwise meager incomes, feeding a rampant black market in surplus arms.[78]

Eritrea, which fought a three-decade war for independence from Ethiopia, has shown that there are opportunities for demobilization and post-conflict rehabilitation to reinforce each other. Many of the former liberation fighters are now engaged in reforestation and soil conservation projects, and involved in rebuilding schools, hospitals, roads, bridges, and other infrastructure. But success is not automatic. Reintegration does not happen "spontaneously," as the Namibian government, for example, had hoped. Without special plans in place to facilitate the process, 57 percent of the discharged Namibian fighters found themselves unemployed.[79]

In Nicaragua, 65,000 Sandinista soldiers and 23,000 Contra rebels were demobilized after the end of the country's devastating civil war. Promises of land, reintegration, other economic assistance, and health services to the demobilized and their families had generated high hopes but failed to materialize in many cases. Many former Contras now live in abject poverty in northern Nicaragua, and severe hardships have led former combatants from both sides to turn to banditry and gun-running, causing the deaths of hundreds of civilians in the early 1990s. Thousands of frustrated ex-combatants regrouped into so-called "Re-Compas" (former Sandinistas) and "Re-Contras" (former rebel fighters). Initially they fought each other, but eventually they came to focus on confronting the government. The government has fought several skirmishes with the rearmed groups, even as it tried to find a negotiated solution and renewed promises of assistance to rebels who lay down their arms. Some rebels moved into designated "peace zones," but others subsequently resumed their armed operations in early 1997 because they lacked confidence in the government's promises.[80]

In southern Africa, extensive demobilization has been

taking place in Zimbabwe, Namibia, Mozambique, South Africa, and Angola. Unfortunately, a common characteristic of all these efforts is the lack of well-planned and well-funded programs to help ex-combatants reintegrate into their communities.[81]

In Mozambique, discharged former combatants were to receive a relatively generous two years' worth of severance pay and were eligible for vocational training provided by the International Labour Organisation. But only a portion of international funding promised for these endeavors became available in timely fashion. Furthermore, as Peter Batchelor of the Center for Conflict Resolution at the University of Cape Town points out, there were no "complementary" programs—such as the provision of seeds and agricultural implements, public work schemes, and the rehabilitation of infrastructure—that would have facilitated reintegration. Not surprisingly, the lack of employment opportunities for ex-fighters led to a rise in crime and violence.[82]

From a pampered institution, the Russian military moved literally to the edge of starvation.

The verdict is still out on Angola's experience. After a failed peacemaking attempt in 1991 that led to new fighting, the government and UNITA rebels struck a new deal in 1994. But demobilization and the formation of a new, joint army are moving at a slow, uncertain pace. By June 1997, some 71,000 UNITA personnel had registered in U.N. demobilization centers; but 26,000 of them deserted, their whereabouts unknown. (After UNITA demobilization is completed, some 30,000 government soldiers are to be discharged as well.) Banditry among ex-combatants is on the rise. On top of all that, questions have arisen as to whether UNITA leader Jonas Savimbi will allow peace to take hold. As many as 30,000 UNITA fighters have apparently been held back from demobilization. Those reporting for discharge not only handed in fewer weapons than expected, but nearly half of those weapons were found to be unserviceable (by implication, the best weapons are being retained). By mid-1997, there were reports that renewed fighting in the country's northeast was gathering momentum.[83]

In the successor states to the former Soviet Union, the state of the armed forces went from one extreme to another: from a pampered and bloated institution that consumed the most precious resources the Soviet state could muster, the military moved literally to the edge of starvation. The size of the armed forces declined from about 3.9 million soldiers in the last years of the Soviet Union to about 2.4 million in 1995 for Russia and the other successor republics. President Yeltsin announced in mid-1997 that he intended to cut the Russian army further, from 1.8 million to 1.2 million. Reducing the military makes eminent sense, particularly for a country whose economy has come close to collapse. Yet the widespread desperation among soldiers, along with an unreliable inventory of weapons and inadequate controls over their whereabouts, has opened a Pandora's box: there is fear that a possibly massive selloff of the Soviet military arsenal is under way, from alleged cases of nuclear weapons-related smuggling to less spectacular, but probably very frequent, deals involving Russia's "conventional" weaponry.[84]

Conditions in the Russian armed forces, particularly for conscripts, are nothing short of appalling. Soldiers are now generally underpaid, undernourished, poorly clothed, and compelled to live in substandard housing. Many soldiers work as laborers to supplement their meager pay; many others have resorted to begging to survive. Indeed, as miserable as prison conditions are in Russia, it would seem that convicts are better off than soldiers, as the *New York Times* recently reported: "Army privates are allotted 5,000 rubles (about 70 cents) a day for food. By contrast, prisoners ...receive 7,750 rubles' worth of food each day."[85]

Beyond tales of individual suffering, there is a more systemic concern. A February 1997 statement by the Council for Foreign and Defense Policy, a private research group in Moscow, warned: "Within the next three years, the army, if it is not reformed, will disappear as such, or it will break up into armed groups that make ends meet through selling arms or robberies, or there could be a military coup, which could grow into dictatorship or civil war." The possibility of factions of the armed forces competing openly and violently is not entirely farfetched. Already, different segments of the armed forces are vying for funds and government favors. In an open letter to the Kremlin that shook the Russian leadership, a Russian general, Lev Rokhlin, contended that the Yeltsin government intentionally impoverished the troops under the command of the Defense Ministry while providing much better support to 260,000 Interior Ministry troops. Rokhlin accused the government of intending to use the Interior Ministry troops as a sort of "Praetorian guard" in the event of popular unrest.[86]

As different as the Russian, African, and Central American experiences are, they have in common at least one factor: the positive trend of shrinking armies is clouded to some extent by the threat of large quantities of arms leaking and dispersing to new conflicts, and former soldiers becoming agents of discontent and instability.

Taking Weapons Out of Circulation

> When a conflict ends ..., arms suppliers take no responsibility for either the cost of disarmament or the impact upon civil societies when disarmament fails. This should change, but change can only happen ... if the international community ... [enforces] the 'polluter pays' principle in this field.
>
> —*Chris Smith, Centre for Defence Studies,*
> *King's College, London, 1996.*[87]

The most immediate challenge in coping with small arms is to reduce the number of weapons that are already in circulation. First, weapons that are now surplus to the needs of armies in industrialized countries will need to be dismantled instead of being sold off cheaply. Second, arms that are

left over at the end of civil wars in developing countries
need to be collected before they fall into the hands of
domestic or international smugglers.

We have only seen the beginnings of a large-scale selloff of surplus weapons among industrialized countries.
According to BICC, eight times as many major weapons still
await disposal as have already been transferred in the post-
cold war era. It may be assumed that a similar situation holds
true with regard to small arms. If they want to prevent the
recirculation of even more massive amounts of used weaponry—and the resulting increase in violence likely to ensue—
governments will need to change their priorities, dismantling surplus stocks instead of selling them off—or risk having them stolen and smuggled. In principle, this should not
be a problem for Western countries, which are offering these
arms at substantial discounts and can afford to forego the
revenue earned. Russia and other former Soviet republics, by
contrast, have inadequate financial resources to destroy surplus arms, and their soldiers have every incentive to sell off
weapons. It is in the Western (and global) interest to assist
Russia in dismantling excess arms. It would also be sensible
to incorporate into any future disarmament agreements an
explicit stipulation that surplus arms be dismantled rather
than just withdrawn from active deployment.

An equally important task is to deal with those arms
that have become surplus with the end of civil wars in Central America, southern Africa, and other regions. Because the
transition to peace has in many cases been accomplished
with the assistance of peacekeeping operations, the United
Nations has become increasingly involved in the post-conflict disarmament of former combatants. The U.N. has also
shown growing interest in the issue of small-arms proliferation generally. In 1992, Secretary-General Boutros-Ghali
called attention to what he termed the need for "microdis-
armament," and established a Panel of Governmental
Experts on Small Arms. A variety of General Assembly and
Security Council resolutions have been passed in recent
years on related issues, reflecting growing concern among

national governments.[88]

Since 1989, several U.N. peacekeeping operations have become involved in disarming ex-combatants. UNIDIR has conducted a "Disarmament and Conflict Resolution" project to evaluate the disarmament experience of 11 U.N. peacekeeping operations, publishing the findings in nine separate volumes in 1995–97. (See Table 6.)[89]

UNIDIR found several recurring problems handicapping these operations. Typically, at the end of a conflict there is no firm or reliable inventory of the total number of weapons in the possession of combatants, so that it is difficult to assess to what extent disarmament is actually taking place. A substantial portion of the weapons handed in by ex-combatants tends to be of inferior quality—by implication the best armaments are retained or hidden. Another difficulty arises from the fact that in countries with civil wars, government and insurgent forces alike often pass out large amounts of small arms to the civilian population. Yet peacekeeping operations either have no mandate to disarm civilians, or they do not have the requisite resources and political backup to do so. In all the U.N. operations, only some of the arms in circulation were collected; in some cases, the collected weapons were destroyed, but in others, many were actually passed on to the new army (integrating government and rebel soldiers) that emerged after a country's peace accord. The volume of arms is often several times larger than needed to outfit these smaller forces. Weak controls and the fact that many soldiers subsist on low salaries are a virtual invitation for stealing and selling arms.

There are thus many lessons to be learned from the peacekeeping experience. One is that disarmament needs to be given higher priority among the array of tasks that peacekeeping missions are expected to carry out. But improving the disarmament performance of peacekeeping operations also requires a general strengthening of the capacity of these missions. This means clearly formulated mandates, properly prepared personnel, sufficient funding, and consistent political support. U.N. peacekeeping has suffered from a wide gap

TABLE 6

U.N. Peacekeeping and Small-Arms Disarmament, Late 1980s and 1990s

Country/Region	Experience of Selected Peacekeeping Operations
Central America	Oversaw voluntary disarmament of the Contra rebels in Nicaragua and Honduras in 1990. Of 15,000 small arms collected, most destroyed. But weapons handed in may present only a small fraction of the total held; many of the collected weapons of inferior quality. A partial success.
El Salvador	Supervised disarmament of FMLN rebels in 1992–93. About 10,000 small-caliber arms and other weapons destroyed. Similar amounts collected from demobilized government soldiers. The U.N. had no mandate to disarm the civilian population; 200,000-300,000 military weapons remain in civilian hands. Limited success.
Mozambique	Collected about 190,000 weapons, mostly of inferior quality and only a tiny fraction of all arms in circulation. No attempt to disarm the civilian population. A limited portion of the collected arms destroyed, the rest transferred to the Mozambican army. Many arms subsequently stolen. Largely a failure.
Somalia	Several ill-considered phases of disarmament, from a failed food-for-guns exchange, to a vendetta-like coercive disarmament campaign against a single Somali warlord, to the abrupt abandonment of any disarmament efforts. A complete failure.
Cambodia	Peace agreement included disarming some 140,000 combatants from different factions. When Khmer Rouge refused to demobilize, the U.N. decided against a coercive strategy. Only one quarter of the combatants were disarmed. The U.N. collected a small amount of weapons, mostly of inferior quality. There may now be more weapons in Cambodia than when the U.N. left the country. Largely a failure.

Sources: See endnote 89.

between what national governments expect these missions to accomplish and what they are prepared to invest in them. Although the United States (and some other U.N. member states) have complained in recent years that peacekeeping missions are too expensive and that the date by which they are completed should be determined at the outset, the experience suggests virtually the opposite: If disarmament of ex-combatants is to be accomplished satisfactorily, it will sometimes take a lengthy commitment of people, equipment, and resources.[90]

Chris Smith suggests countries neighboring a nation emerging from war as a possible source of funding; they could be expected to have a natural interest in ensuring the success of peace and disarmament efforts because they would reap the repercussions of failure: influx of refugees, arms smuggling, and general instability. But Smith also argues that the original arms suppliers who now take no responsibility for the consequences of their sales should be made to fund peace efforts, in what would be the equivalent of the 'polluter pays' principle. This is no doubt a fair proposal, but the trick is to devise a political formula to implement it. As with any imaginative new idea, the first task is to popularize it to build support.[91]

There are additional lessons. A greater effort needs to be made to ascertain the quality and quantity of weapons present in a country to which peacekeepers are dispatched. More than before, peace accords will need to encompass detailed inventories of the arsenals held by the different parties to a conflict. Once the disarmament and demobilization of combatants gets under way, it needs to take place in a manner that no faction perceives an advantage or disadvantage to itself. And once the weapons are collected, a greater effort must be made to place them in secure storage until they can be dismantled, or at least to render them unusable as quickly as possible.

Experience shows that the more time passes before disarmament is implemented, the more likely it is that the parties to the conflict will begin to renege on their commitment to disarm. This points to the need to proceed swiftly with any disarmament operations. But if the antagonists fail to live up to their promises, the question arises whether disarmament should be pursued in a more coercive, rather than a consensual, manner. As experience demonstrates, both choices have their pitfalls. In a UNIDIR study, analyst Fred Tanner argues that "coercive disarmament measures can only be used in carefully defined circumstances and not as a general rule." In other words, they need to be limited either to geographically designated zones (safety zones), related to a certain type of conduct (such as the open and hostile display of weapons), or focused on certain types of weapons. Tanner adds that coercive measures should be used only in circumstances where the parties can be held accountable for non-compliance; that they should involve only minimal use of force, not full-scale combat; and that peacekeepers need to preserve impartiality and cooperation with the parties on the "strategic" level.[92]

In addition to disarmament efforts in the context of peacekeeping operations, several countries have tried so-called gun buy-back programs. Even some nations that have not had recent wars on their soil have gone this route in an effort to reduce the number of weapons in circulation. Under the buy-back schemes, individuals are encouraged to turn in arms voluntarily in return for compensation. (See Table 7.)[93]

The experience has been quite varied, teaching important lessons that will help to improve and finetune future programs. Several observers agree that one possible pitfall of buy-backs is that monetary compensation in return for guns may provide an incentive to steal guns in order to turn them in for cash. Edward Laurance warns that "without stringent requirements on the quality ... and quantity of guns, funds can soon be depleted by exploitative private gun owners and dealers who use the exchange of outdated and poor quality weapons to purchase newer and higher quality firearms." Pricing can be the crucial factor: at compensation levels that are too far below the black-market value, few firearms will be turned in; but at levels that are too high, the black market

TABLE 7

Selected Examples of Gun-Buyback Programs, 1990s

Country	Observation
Colombia	Nationwide food-for-guns program established (those with legally owned weapons receive a check for the value of the weapon). Bogota cash-for-weapons program helped cause a sharp drop in 1997 homicides.
El Salvador	Goods-for-guns program run by Patriotic Movement Against Crime collected close to 5,000 weapons during 1996 and early 1997. Yet the acquisition of new weapons—1,500 registered arms per month—far outpaces this effort. Another program (sponsored by New York-based Guns for Goods), exchanges vouchers to buy food and clothes for guns in three cities. In both cases, lack of funding limits effectiveness.
Nicaragua	Buy-back program incorporated cash and food incentives and an Italian-sponsored micro-enterprise program. During 1992–93, about 64,000 weapons were bought back and 78,000 confiscated, and all were destroyed. 250,000 pieces of ammunition were also collected. Total cost $6 million.
Haiti	A U.S. Army gun buy-back program paid cash for functional weapons and confiscated non-functional ones. By March 1995, more than 33,000 weapons taken in, at a cost of $1.9 million. Weapons in good condition were passed on to the Haitian police, the remainder melted down.
Mozambique	A program sponsored by the Christian Council of Mozambique allows people to exchange weapons for cows, sewing machines, plows, and other goods. Program began in 1996 with a $1.2 million grant.
Australia	The massacre of 35 people by a gunman in April 1996 prompted the government to enact a broadly supported ban on automatic and semi-automatic weapons. More than 600,000 of perhaps up to 2 million arms were handed in. The government paid $217 million in compensation.

Sources: See endnote 93.

will be stimulated. Particularly in developing countries where many ex-fighters are expected to return to homes in rural areas, Peter Batchelor points out, buy-back programs that provide food or agricultural implements are more appropriate than programs that offer cash for weapons. Generally speaking, buy-back schemes will tend to be more successful if they are embedded in broader community programs.[94]

Firearm owners need to feel secure that turning in an illegally held weapon will not expose them to retribution. A "no-questions-asked" policy may work best. Governments from the Dominican Republic, to Lesotho, to Sri Lanka, have instituted so-called "amnesty" programs in recent years, permitting unlicensed or otherwise illegal firearms to be turned in during a certain period of time without fear of prosecution. Britain has made use of the amnesty approach on four different occasions, in 1965, 1968, 1988, and 1996, collecting a total of more than 130,000 firearms.[95]

The tools required to reduce the number of weapons in circulation are not in much question. What needs attention and improvement, however, is the ways in which they are wielded. The experience of the last few years has shown that programs to collect arms will need considerable refinement and more substantial financial and political support if they are to succeed.

Adopting the "Orphans" of Arms Control

> The greatest hurdle to overcome in controlling the trade in light arms is not powerful *lawbreakers* but weak *lawmakers*.
> —Aaron Karp, Old Dominion University, Virginia.[96]

Small arms and light weapons are the orphans of arms control. Throughout the Cold War years, arms control and disarmament efforts have focused exclusively on major weapons systems. Although this has begun to change in recent years, there are no internationally accepted norms or standards regarding small arms; their production, trade, and possession still remain essentially unmonitored and unregulated.[97]

The tools and assumptions of traditional arms control, focused as they are on nuclear and major conventional arms, and tailored to the needs and circumstances of Cold War protagonists in North America, Russia, and Europe, have little relevance for dealing with the spread of small arms and the peculiar set of internal conflicts in which they are used to devastating effect. East-West-style arms control presupposes a stable relationship between opposing governments. Although the United States and the Soviet Union were highly antagonistic, there was considerable confidence that agreements hammered out by arms negotiators would indeed be carried out, and that even arcane details of compliance could be clarified between the opposing sides. In contrast, most contemporary conflicts involve a tangle of forces with conflicting claims of authority and divergent levels of accountability.

For these reasons, focusing on allowed numbers of weapons to be deployed by one or the other side—the central tenet of old-style arms control—makes little sense. The challenge is not finding some magical balance-of-power formula to arrive at "stable" levels of armaments fielded by opposing sides (something that in reality is seldom achieved even in the realm of major weapons arms control) as it is sharply curtailing the general availability of arms. To tackle the challenge of small arms, a multitude of approaches can be pursued. These include creating greater transparency, restricting both legal and illegal international transfers, establishing restrictions on new production, and banning particular types of weapons.

However, better access to data is clearly the most immediate need if policymakers are not to move forward blindly. One way to proceed is to establish a register of small arms, either on a global or regional basis. This could be modeled on the existing U.N. Register of Conventional Arms. Since 1993, the U.N. has published an annual register of imports and exports of seven types of major weapons systems, based on voluntary submissions of data by member states. Over the years, it has found increasing acceptance as a growing number of governments participate. Unlike the existing register, a small-arms register (or set of regional registers) might also encompass information on national production and stockpiles and provide pre-notification of pending transfers rather than after-the-fact information. The idea of a regional register has been discussed by the Organization of American States (OAS) and by the Association of South East Asian Nations (ASEAN).[98]

Greater transparency would allow improved restrictions on questionable arms transfers. One such recommendation is the adoption of a "code of conduct" by national governments. Former Costa Rican President and Nobel Peace Prize recipient Oscar Arias has initiated a campaign for a global code. Under his proposal, weapons would not be made available to countries that fail to meet the following criteria: compliance with international human rights standards and humanitarian law, respect for democratic norms, adherence to international arms embargoes and military sanctions, and participation in the existing U.N. arms register. Nor could weapons be sold to countries that engage in armed aggression. With the support of several other Nobel Peace laureates, Dr. Arias formally released his code on May 29, 1997, and plans to present it to the U.N. General Assembly as the first step in a process that is aimed at concluding an international treaty embodying the code's principles.[99]

In the United States, a coalition of grassroots groups has waged a campaign for a similar code for several years. Several legislative efforts in the U.S. Congress failed in 1995 and 1996. In June 1997, a watered-down version was passed in the House of Representatives. Instead of an airtight prohibition against arms sales to countries that fail to live up to the code's provisions, the President could seek a waiver and Congress would have eight months to block or condition the request. Similar legislation has been introduced in the Senate.[100]

Support for a code is growing elsewhere. Some 15 former and current Latin American heads of state endorsed the idea in 1997, and it is under discussion in southern Africa. In Europe, a growing number of national governments, parliaments, individual parliamentarians, and grassroots groups have called for a code of conduct. Indeed, the European Parliament endorsed the idea in September 1992 and again in February 1994. The European Council of Ministers and the Organization on Security and Co-operation in Europe (OSCE) separately agreed on sets of criteria to govern arms exports of member states. Yet their members still differ widely on how the criteria should be interpreted, and governments are not yet legally bound by them. In Britain, the new Labour government has shown greater willingness than its predecessor to bar sales to governments with poor human rights records.[101]

In addition to restricting governmentally approved sales, a greater effort is also needed to clamp down on illegal transfers. Although it may appear futile to try to restrict clandestine flows of small arms, "controls do not have to stop every gun and bullet," as Aaron Karp has pointed out. It may be sufficient to block the biggest transfers and interrupt the most important transfer routes. And such efforts might particularly focus on flows of ammunition, argues Edward Laurance: not only is the capacity to manufacture ammunition less widespread than that to produce the small weapons themselves (making transfers a potential choke point), but because ammunition is heavy and bulky, it is less easy to transfer clandestinely.[102]

Restricting illicit transfers of weapons and ammunition alike would involve enhancing national customs controls and other measures to improve the monitoring of cross-border flows of goods. But arms traffickers will be able to circumvent strict regulations in one country so long as others have weak laws. Hence, there is a need to harmonize export regulations, and to step up international cooperation, for instance by establishing shared databases on known or suspected traffickers and illicit end users. Lora Lumpe of the Federation of American Scientists has proposed creation of an international registry of authorized buyers, though it might be difficult to arrive at a consensus in defining legitimate recipients.[103]

Several regional efforts to counter gun-smuggling are under way. At the urging of Jamaica, the United States has agreed to participate in talks with Caribbean countries; Jamaican authorities contend that a rising crime rate is being fueled by weapons smuggled in from the United States. Similar concerns led Mexico in the fall of 1996 to propose a convention against illicit firearms trafficking; the OAS is now preparing a draft. Central American governments, meanwhile, are expected to ratify an agreement to enhance exchange of information and inspection of exports. In southern Africa, a tripartite accord was signed between South Africa, Swaziland, and Mozambique in June 1993 in an attempt to deal with the problem of illegal arms flows into South Africa. In January 1995, South Africa and Mozambique signed an agreement to facilitate cross-border police cooperation to track down illegal weaponry; by late 1997, the accord had led to three joint operations in which several thousand small arms and several million rounds of ammunition were seized and destroyed. The success of this cooperation is likely to lead to similar missions between South Africa and other countries in the region. Finally, the Council of Ministers of the European Union launched an initiative in June 1997 to develop a common database on illicit arms trafficking, strengthen collective efforts to prevent and combat such transfers, and assist other countries in similar endeavors.[104]

Restricting the flow of weaponry without addressing the issue of continued production, however, is like stopping the flow of water from a hose by holding the nozzle closed; before too long, the water pressure will cause leaks. The longer large-scale production continues, the greater the future supply of weapons and ammunition whose whereabouts and use will be of concern. And yet, reining in production is as difficult politically as its need is obvious.

One obstacle is the "addiction to war industries," as R.T. Naylor puts it. Although small weapons do not figure as prominently as major weapons in the corporate drive for profits and the governmental interest in boosting export revenues, this addiction will be an impediment as long as there are no effective programs to provide economic alternatives to work forces and communities dependent on arms production.[105]

Skeptics will argue that there are simply too many factories or small workshops engaged in small-arms manufacturing to make a ban or sharp reductions in production possible. It is true that the number of small gunsmiths, including individuals who make crude, home-made weapons, is large and diverse enough to defy any attempt at totally controlling output. But the success of restricting production rests on reaching those factories that are capable of churning out large volumes of more advanced types of small arms and ammunition.

The longer large-scale production continues, the greater the future supply of arms whose whereabouts will be of concern.

On the demand side, another problem is that a considerable portion of small-arms production is destined for such legitimate users as national police forces and—because of weak domestic gun control laws—ordinary citizens. The belief that police forces have to have sufficient firepower to deter criminals (and therefore have to engage in a domestic "arms race" of sorts) or that the right to bear arms is a hallmark of personal freedom is deeply entrenched in many societies. Charlton Heston, a well-known former actor and now a senior official for the U.S. National Rifle Association, asserted in a recent speech that the right to bear arms was "more essential" than the constitutional guarantee of freedom of speech and other civil liberties.[106]

Initially, attempts to restrict small arms may best be focused on the most "objectionable" types of weapons, those least likely to be found in the hands of the general population.

Domestic gun control efforts in many countries have zeroed in on possession of assault rifles and other automatic and semi-automatic firearms. Britain, Australia, and Canada are among the countries that have recently tightened their laws, but the lack of effective regulation in other countries, and the ease with which weapons are smuggled across borders can undermine these efforts. Laws addressing firearms possession may be condemned to ineffectiveness unless production and trade are confronted as well.[107]

Internationally, growing attention is directed at efforts to ban the production, transfer, and use of anti-personnel landmines—weapons that have long been considered particularly cruel in their effects. For many years they were covered by a weak international treaty, the "Convention on the Prohibition or Restrictions on the Use of Certain Conventional Weapons Which May Be Deemed to be Excessively Injurious or to Have Indiscriminate Effects." Although the CCW Convention, as it is often referred to, was strengthened somewhat in early 1996, the revisions fell far short of what was needed to truly confront the global landmine crisis.[108]

Instead, since 1992, an international grassroots campaign—now comprising more than 1,000 human rights groups and other NGOs in 60 countries—has made considerable progress in delegitimizing anti-personnel mines and pressing governments to move toward a complete ban on these weapons. A growing number of national governments have taken their own unilateral steps: as of July 1997, 50 countries had declared a ban or moratorium on the export of mines; 34 decided to suspend or renounce any future national use; 33 of those that once manufactured mines moved to prohibit continued production; and 19 announced that they were going to destroy existing stockpiles.[109]

With a rising number of countries supporting an international ban, the Canadian government invited other states to a conference in Ottawa in October 1996 to kick off a concerted effort among like-minded governments to draft a formal treaty outlawing the production, stockpiling, transfer, and use of anti-personnel mines. The "Ottawa process" led

to the adoption of treaty language by almost 100 governments in September 1997; the treaty will be open for signa-
ture in December 1997.[110]

Several countries opposed the Ottawa process, particularly China and Russia, both of which are major producers
and insist that mines are militarily indispensable. The
United States, meanwhile, joined the negotiations belatedly
and sought, unsuccessfully, several exceptions that would
have undermined a true ban. The Clinton Administration
ultimately decided that it would not sign the treaty (although the United States had not exported mines for about
five years). U.S. support would have reinforced the emerging
global norm against anti-personnel mines, increasing the
pressure on other holdouts—Russia, China, India, Pakistan,
and Israel, among others—to reconsider.[111]

It is true that the particularly gruesome and indiscriminate nature of landmines—qualities that may not apply as
clearly to other small weapons—has helped the ban campaign to succeed. But the experience nevertheless offers
broader lessons. The first is that through persistent and ded-
icated work, NGOs can succeed in raising an issue—stigma-
tizing reliance on particularly objectionable weapons—that
otherwise would not be on any government's agenda.

Second, because NGOs tend to approach weapons issues
from a different vantage point than governments, they often
support more far-reaching measures. Out of political and
strategic considerations, governments generally have an interest in regulating, but not banning, certain weapons, and
in controlling, not stopping, their production. The actions
of many grassroots organizations, on the other hand, tend
to be motivated by social, environmental, or humanitarian
concerns.

Third, anti-landmine NGOs have been able to form a
working coalition with the governments of several small
powers—Canada, Austria, Norway, Belgium, and South
Africa among them—whose actions came to be guided
increasingly by humanitarian, not by military-strategic considerations. With the help of intense media scrutiny, these

governments were able to take the initiative in international diplomacy. The Ottawa process may indeed herald the beginnings of a new inter-governmental process, in which not the big powers but the smaller powers, in concert with NGOs, lead the way.[112]

Fourth, the anti-landmine campaign has also made clear that the challenge of small arms knows no borders. Whether it be the spread of landmines, assault rifles, or any other small weapon, countermeasures can only hope to be effective if they are taken in a context of international—and preferably global—cooperation. The efforts of a single country or small group of nations are too easily circumvented by far-flung networks to produce and trade small arms.

The final key to change is public awareness. A strong constituency for alternative policies can be brought to life by making clear the horrendous effects of the virtually unlimited availability of small arms—the suffering of victims, the endless cycle of violence, the persistent insecurity. Once people understand the repercussions, the political dynamic changes: what was previously unthinkable begins to come within reach. For a long time, small arms and light weapons have escaped thorough scrutiny; their ubiquitous presence has been accepted as a necessary evil or even welcomed as a guarantor of security and a symbol of freedom. But this is beginning to change as growing numbers of people realize that excessive quantities of small arms can have devastating consequences. Progress will not come easily, given that small arms are already so widely available and that gun lobbies and other vested interests can be expected to work hard to prevent change. Nevertheless, as the anti-landmine campaign demonstrates, change is possible.

Notes

Note on electronic sources:

Several of the references for this paper were obtained from on-line sources, either from World Wide Web sites or from computer conferences in the APC (Association for Progressive Communications) system. The U.S. component of the APC system—Econet—is maintained by the Institute for Global Communications in San Francisco, California.

1. The news picture was reprinted, for instance, in the *New York Times* on 23 March 1997.

2. Aaron Karp, "Small Arms—The New Major Weapons," in Jeffrey Boutwell, Michael T. Klare, and Laura W. Reed, eds., *Lethal Commerce: The Global Trade in Small Arms and Light Weapons* (Cambridge, MA: Committee on International Security Studies, American Academy of Arts and Sciences, 1995); 90 percent figure from Sverre Lodgaard, "Preface," in Estanislao Angel Zawels, Stephen John Stedman, Donald C.F. Daniel, et al., *Managing Arms in Peace Processes: The Issues*, United Nations Institute for Disarmament Research (UNIDIR) Disarmament and Conflict Resolution Project (New York and Geneva: U.N., 1996).

3. Governments publish limited data, but independent researchers have begun to gather information. For example, Michael Klare and David Andersen have compiled fairly extensive data for Latin America. See their *A Scourge of Guns: The Diffusion of Small Arms and Light Weapons in Latin America* (Washington, D.C.: Arms Sales Monitoring Project, Federation of American Scientists (FAS), August 1996). 500 million estimate from Jasjit Singh, "Introduction," in Jasjit Singh, ed., *Light Weapons and International Security* (Delhi: Indian Pugwash Society and British American Security Information Council, December 1995).

4. U.N. "Report of the Panel of Governmental Experts on Small Arms," New York, July 1997, (pre-publication version).

5. For detailed discussion, see Michael Renner, *Fighting for Survival: Environmental Decline, Social Conflict, and the New Age of Insecurity* (New York: W.W. Norton & Company, 1996).

6. Jeffrey Boutwell, Michael T. Klare, and Laura W. Reed, "Introduction," in Boutwell et al., op. cit. note 2; Michael T. Klare, "The New Arms Race: Light Weapons and International Security," *Current History*, April 1997, <http://www.currenthistory.com/Klare.html>.

7. "Small arms and light weapons" is the commonly accepted term in the literature. For convenience's sake, this paper will use the terms "small arms" and "small weapons." Definitional issues are discussed by Michael Klare,

"Stemming the Lethal Trade in Small Arms and Light Weapons," *Issues in Science and Technology*, fall 1995, by Karp, op. cit. note 2, by Edward Laurance, *The New Field of Micro-Disarmament: Addressing the Proliferation and Buildup of Small Arms and Light Weapons*, BICC Brief 7 (Bonn: Bonn International Center for Conversion (BICC), September 1996), and by Swadesh Rana, *Small Arms and Intra-State Conflicts*, UNIDIR Research Paper no. 34 (Geneva and New York: United Nations Institute for Disarmament Research, 1995), Appendix I.

8. Klare, op. cit. note 7. If somewhat heavier arms, such as crew-served weapons like heavy machine guns and mortars, are included, the $3 billion figure may well double.

9. Ibid.

10. Laurance, op. cit. note 7; Christopher Smith, "Light Weapons and the International Arms Trade," in Christopher Smith, Peter Batchelor, and Jakkie Potgieter, *Small Arms Management and Peacekeeping in Southern Africa*, UNIDIR Disarmament and Conflict Resolution Project (New York and Geneva: U.N., 1996).

11. Rachel Brett and Margaret McCallin, *Children: The Invisible Soldiers* (Växjö, Sweden: Rädda Barnen - Swedish Save the Children, 1996); U.N. General Assembly, "Impact of Armed Conflict on Children. Note by the Secretary-General," A/51/306, 26 August 1996; Thalif Deen, "Child Soldier Ranks Rise with Cheap, Easy Arms," *Jane's Defense Weekly*, 20 November 1996.

12. Natalie J. Goldring, British-American Security Information Council (BASIC), "Bridging the Gap: Light and Major Conventional Weapons in Recent Conflicts," paper prepared for the annual meeting of the International Studies Association, Toronto, Ontario, 18-21 March 1997, retrieved from BASIC Web Site, <http://www.igc.apc.org/basic/isa97.html>, viewed 17 April 1997; Michael Klare, Hampshire College, e-mail message to author, 2 September 1997.

13. Smith, op. cit. note 10; Rana, op. cit. note 7; BICC, *Conversion Survey 1997: Global Disarmament and Disposal of Surplus Arms* (New York: Oxford University Press, 1997).

14. Klaus Jürgen Gantzel and Torsten Schwinghammer, *Die Kriege nach dem Zweiten Weltkrieg 1945 bis 1992. Daten und Tendenzen* (Münster and Hamburg, Germany: Lit Verlag, 1995); Dietrich Jung, Klaus Schlichte, and Jens Siegelberg, *Das Kriegsgeschehen 1995. Daten und Tendenzen der Kriege und bewaffneten Konflikte im Jahr 1995* (Bonn: Stiftung Entwicklung und Frieden, 1996). Definitional and methodological questions, along with the lack of reliable information in some cases, explain why different analysts report slightly different numbers of armed conflicts in progress. Researchers at the University of Uppsala, Sweden—another widely used source—recorded 35 ongoing wars in 1995 and 36 in 1996. See Peter Wallensteen and Margareta Sollenberg, "Armed Conflicts, Conflict Termination and Peace Agreements, 1989-1996," *Journal of Peace Research*, vol. 34, no. 3; Margareta Sollenberg, ed., *States in Armed Conflict 1995*, Uppsala University, Department of Peace and Conflict Research, Report No. 43, 1996. Project Ploughshares, a Canadian research group, reports a higher number—44 armed conflicts— for 1995. See Project Ploughshares, *Armed Conflicts Report 1996* (Waterloo, Canada: Institute of Peace and Conflict Studies, Conrad Grebel College, 1996). Figure 1 is based on Gantzel and Schwinghammer, and Jung et al., both op. cit. this note.

15. Wallensteen and Sollenberg, op. cit. note 14; number of child soldiers from the U.N. Children's Fund (UNICEF), *The State of the World's Children 1996* (New York: Oxford University Press, 1996); conflicts with child soldiers from Brett and McCallin, op. cit. note 11, and from Project Ploughshares, op. cit. note 14.

16. Wallensteen and Sollenberg, op. cit. note 14; war-related deaths computed from Ruth Leger Sivard with Arlette Brauer, Lora Lumpe, and Paul Walker, *World Military and Social Expenditures 1996* (Washington, D.C.: World Priorities, 1996). Figure 2 presents data in 5-year periods because there is no reliable information on the annual death toll. It is a Worldwatch computation based on data in Sivard, op. cit. this note. The data underlying the figure have been calculated on the basis of the total number of persons killed in each individual war; where wars have straddled two or more 5-year periods, the total number of deaths was divided into equal portions for the periods of time in question. For example, the Israeli invasion and partial occupation of Lebanon is estimated to have killed 63,000 people in 1982–90. This was broken down into 28,000 for the 1981–85 period and 35,000 for the 1986–90 period. Milton Leitenberg of the University of Maryland contends that the death toll since 1945 has been as high as 44 million. Most of the difference arises from his extraordinarily high mortality figures for revolutionary violence within China from the 1940s to the 1970s. See Milton Leitenberg, "Humanitarian Intervention and Other International Initiatives to Enforce Peace," Center for International and Security Studies at Maryland (CISSM), University of Maryland, College Park, MD, February 1993.

17. Dan Smith, *War, Peace and Third World Development*, Human Development Report Office, Occasional Paper No. 16, U.N. Development Programme, New York, 1993; Jung et al., op. cit. note 14.

18. Michael T. Klare, "Light Weapons Diffusion and Global Violence in the Post-Cold War Era," in Singh, op. cit. note 3, "Kenya Cattle Rustlers Kill 31," Associated Press, 22 September 1997.

19. Klare and Andersen, op. cit. note 3; "The Backlash in Latin America," *Economist*, 30 November 1996; Jacklyn Cock, "A Sociological Account of Light Weapons Proliferation in Southern Africa," in Singh, op. cit. note 3.

20. Michael T. Klare, "The Global Trade in Light Weapons and the International System in the Post-Cold War Era," in Boutwell et al., op. cit. note 2.

21. Daniel Gallik, ed., World Military Expenditures and Arms Transfers electronic database, U.S. Arms Control and Disarmament Agency, Washington, D.C., computer diskette provided to author, 20 January 1997; armed opposition figure calculated from International Institute for Strategic Studies (IISS), *The Military Balance 1996/97* (London: Oxford University Press, 1996). Among the countries with large armed opposition groups, IISS has no data for Algeria, Burundi, Chad, India, Mexico, Pakistan, Russia, Senegal, and Zaire. The Stockholm International Peace Research Institute (SIPRI) puts armed opposition forces in Chechnya at 12,000-20,000 in 1995 and at 5,000-10,000 in 1996; Margareta Sollenberg and Peter Wallensteen, "Major Armed Conflicts," in SIPRI, *SIPRI Yearbook 1996. Armaments, Disarmament and International Security* (New York: Oxford University Press, 1996), and Margareta Sollenberg and Peter Wallensteen, "Major Armed Conflicts," in SIPRI, *SIPRI Yearbook 1997. Armaments, Disarmament and International Security* (New York: Oxford University Press, 1997).

22. Alex de Waal, "Contemporary Warfare in Africa," *IDS Bulletin*, vol. 27, no. 3.

23. Elizabeth Rubin, "An Army of One's Own," *Harper's*, February 1997; "Papua New Guinea: Line in the Sand," *Economist*, 29 March 1997.

24. James Brooke, "Police/Security Partnerships: Privatization Models that Impace [sic] Crime," *CJ Online the Americas*, <http://www.acsp.uic.edu/oicj/pubs/cja/090211.htm>, viewed 22 July 1997; industry growth expectation and firepower of private guards from Mike Zielinski, "Armed and Dangerous: Private Police on the March," *Covert Action Quarterly*, <http://caq.com/CAQ54p.police.html>, viewed 21 July 1997; 2 million already reached from David H. Baley and Clifford Shearing, "The Future of Policing," *Law & Society Review*, vol. 30, no. 3; historical trends from Les Johnston, *The Rebirth of Private Policing* (London and New York: Routledge, 1992). In addition to these sources, Table 1 is based on Cock, op. cit. note 19; on Jeff Builta, Office of International Criminal Justice, "South Africa: Crime on the Increase," *CJ Online Europe*, <http://www.acsp.uic.edu/OICJ/PUBS/CJE/060101.htm>, viewed 22 July 1997; on U.N., "The Fourth United Nations Survey of Crime Trends and Operations of Criminal Justice Systems," <http://www.ifs.univie.ac.at/~unjin/bpolice/totalpol.txt>, viewed 28 August 1997, on Daniel Garcia-Peña Jaramillo, "Light Weapons and Internal Conflict in Colombia," in Boutwell et al., op. cit., note 2, and on Gallik, op. cit. note 21; "Los Angeles Police to Carry Assault Rifles," Reuter, 17 September 1997; "SWAT Scrutiny," Newshour with Jim Lehrer Transcript, Public Television (PBS), 23 September 1997, <http://www.pbs.org/newshour/bb/military/july-dec97/gun_9-23.html>.

25. "The Backlash in Latin America," op. cit. note 19; current U.S. spending from Zielinski, op. cit. note 24; projection to year 2000 from Morgan O. Reynolds, "Using the Private Sector to Deter Crime," *The Journal of Social, Political and Economic Studies*, summer 1994.

26. Zielinski, op. cit. note 24.

27. Laurance, op. cit. note 7.

28. Statement from "Ramos Orders Crackdown on Gun-runners," *The Straits Times Interactive*, 22 April 1997, <http://straitstimes.asia1.com/>.

29. 500 million figure from Singh, op. cit. note 3; Terry J. Gander, ed., *Jane's Infantry Weapons 1996-97* (London: Jane's Information Group, 1997).

30. "Russia: Kalashnikov Anniversary," *Omri Daily Digest*, 21 February 1997; standard AK-47 black-market price from BICC, op. cit. note 13; price of AK-47 in Uganda and northern Kenya from U.N. General Assembly, op. cit. note 11.

31. Prashant Dikshit, "Internal Conflict and Role of Light Weapons," in Singh, op. cit. note 3; U.N., op. cit. note 4; "Russia: Kalashnikov Anniversary," op. cit. note 30; "Counterfeit Weapons Flood World Arms Market," *The Press* (Christchurch, New Zealand), 3 July 1997; BICC, op. cit. note 13.

32. U.N. Commission on Crime Prevention and Criminal Justice, "Draft United Nations International Study on Firearm Regulation," E/CN.15/ 1997/CRP.6, Vienna, 25 April 1997.

33. Ibid.; Canada from John C. Thompson, *Misfire: The Black Market and Gun Control*, Mackenzie Institute Occasional Paper (Toronto, May 1995).

34. Number of gun dealers from Klare and Andersen, op. cit. note 3; number of McDonald's outlets from Customer Service Department, McDonald's Corporation Head Office, Oak Brook, IL, discussion with Daniel Schwartz, Worldwatch Institute, 3 September 1997; Justice Department from Pierre Thomas, "Study Finds Gun Ownership Common But Less Widespread," *Washington Post*, 6 May 1997; NRA figure from National Rifle Association, "1997 NRA Firearms Fact Card," <http://www.nra.org/research/NRA-FFACT.html>, viewed 2 August 1997; FBI from Katharine Q. Seelye, "NRA Turns to World Stage to Fight Gun Control," *New York Times*, 2 April 1997; annual production and availability from American Firearms Network (Amfire), "Civilian Firearms - Production, Import & Export 1899-1989," <http://www.amfire.com/afistatistics/production2.html>, viewed 2 August 1997, and from Amfire, "Firearms Production 1973-1994," <http://www. amfire.com/afistatistics/production.html>, viewed 2 August 1997; annual theft from Philip J. Cook and Jens Ludwig, "Guns in America: National Survey on Private Ownership and Use of Firearms," *NIJ Research in Brief*, May 1997, <http://libfind.unl.edu:2020/alpha/National_Institute_of_ Justice.html>; U.S. allowing assault weapons ownership from Jeff Brazil and

Steve Berry, "Australia's Answer to Carnage: A Strict Law," *Los Angeles Times*, 27 August 1997, <http://www.latimes.com/outgunned/weapon4a.htm>; share of assault weapons from Jeff Brazil and Steve Berry, "Crackdown on Assault Weapons Has Missed Mark," *Los Angeles Times*, 24 August 1997, <http://www.latimes.com/outgunned/weapon1a.htm>.

35. Catherine Foster, "Nations Around the World Try to Get a Grip on Guns," *Christian Science Monitor*, 15 May 1996; "Drugs Make for Murder Metropolis," *Financial Times*, 10 April 1996.

36. Fred Weir, "Russians Arming Themselves," *Hindustan Times*, 12 March 1997; "Russia: Interior Minister Advocates Tighter Army Gun Control," Moscow Radiostantsiya Ekho Moskvy in (Foreign Broadcast Information Service) *FBIS Daily Report*, FBIS-EEU-97-108, 18 April 1997; Mitchell Landsberg, "Gun Ownership Soars in Russia," Associated Press, 12 May 1997.

37. Christopher Louise, "The Social Impacts of Light Weapons Availability and Proliferation," Discussion Paper No. 59, U.N. Research Institute for Social Development, Geneva, March 1995; comparisons of gun killings in the United States with other industrialized countries from Brazil and Berry, "Australia's Answer ...," op. cit. note 34.

38. Salvadorans killed since 1992 from Klare and Andersen, op. cit. note 3; people killed during the war from Sivard, op. cit. note 16.

39. Larry Rohter, "In U.S. Deportation Policy, a Pandora's Box," *New York Times*, 10 August 1997.

40. *Dialogo Centroamericano*, January 1997 (newsletter published by the Centro para la Paz of the Arias Foundation for Peace and Human Progress, San José, Costa Rica), Klare and Andersen, op. cit. note 3; Laurance, op. cit. note 7.

41. Cock, op. cit. note 19.

42. Ibid.

43. Ibid.; Smith, op. cit. note 10; "Thousands of Illegal Weapons Still Flood into Northern KwaZulu," *The Cape Town Star*, 24 March 1997, <http://www2.inc.co.za/Archives>.

44. "Mozambique is Drowning in the Weapons of Decades of War," *The Cape Town Star*, 24 March 1997, <http://www2.inc.co.za/Archives>; Brian Latham, "Mozambique: Illegal Weapons Trade Threatens Security," *Africa Information* Afrique, 6 March 1995, retrieved from <http://csf.Colorado.EDU:70/00/ipe/Themat...ique/1995/950304.moz.Illegal_Weapon_Trade>, viewed 27 May 1997; Cock, op. cit. note 19; Suzanne Daley, "In Mozambique, Guns for Plowshares and Bicycles," *New York Times*, 2 March 1997.

45. "Police Carry Out Civilian Disarmament Operation in Luanda," Luanda Radio Nacional Network in *FBIS Daily Report,* FBIS-AFR-97-026, 7 February 1997; Gumisai Mutume, "Haven of Peace Threatened by Arms," *Electronic Mail & Guardian* (South Africa), 26 January 1997, <http://www. mg.co.za/mg/news>.

46. European Parliament, "Report of the Committee on Development and Cooperation on Anti-Personnel Landmines: A Murderous Impediment to Development" (Rapporteur: Tony Cunningham), 21 June 1995.

47. Production and other statistics have been compiled from a broad variety of sources, including: Kenneth Anderson, Director, The Arms Project of Human Rights Watch, Statement before the U.S. Senate Appropriations Committee, Subcommittee on Foreign Operations, Hearing on the Global Landmine Crisis, Washington, D.C., 13 May 1994; U.N. Department of Humanitarian Affairs, *Humanitarian Affairs,* April 1996; International Committee of the Red Cross (ICRC) Web site, <http://www.icrc.org/ icrcnews/4796.htm#6>, viewed 24 June 1997; U.N., "UNHCR Calls for International Ban on Land Mines," Press Release REF/1084, 26 May 1994; Human Rights Watch/Arms Project and Physicians for Human Rights, *Landmines: A Deadly Legacy* (New York: Human Rights Watch, October 1993).

48. Number of mines scattered from ICRC, <http://www.icrc.org/ icrcnews/476a.htm>, viewed 24 June 1997; mine retrieval and laying from U.N. General Assembly, "Assistance in Mine Clearance. Report of the Secretary-General," A/49/357, 6 September 1994. Table 2 is based on Human Rights Watch, op. cit. note 47, on ICRC, <http://www.icrc.org/ icrcnews/491e.htm>, viewed 24 June 1997, on Population Reference Bureau, "1996 World Population Data Sheet," Washington, D.C., June 1996, and on *The New York Times Atlas of the World, Third Revised Concise Edition* (New York: Times Books, 1992).

49. ICRC, *Anti-Personnel Landmines—Friend or Foe?* posted on ICRC Web site, <http://www.icrc.org/unicc/icrcnews/>, 28 March 1996; Victims since 1975 and civilian share from James Grant, Executive Director, UNICEF, and Cyrus Vance and Herbert A. Okun, Statements before Hearing on the Global Landmine Crisis, op. cit. note 47; annual victims from ICRC, <http:// www.icrc.org/icrcnews/476a.htm>, viewed 24 June 1997, and from "U.S. Sees Rising Deaths, Injuries from Landmines," Reuter, 7 August 1997, retrieved from San Jose Mercury Web site, <http:www.merc.com/ stories/cgi/story.cgi?id=4330503-2b7>; doubling of victims from Centers for Disease Control and Prevention (CDC), National Center for Environmental Health, "Landmine-Related Injuries, 1993–1996," APC electronic computer conference <igc:disarm.armstra>, posted 8 August 1997; conservative estimate from Robert Windrem, NBC News, "How Bad Is the Problem?" <http://www.msnbc.com/news/110411.asp>, 16 September 1997; Cambodia from U.N. General Assembly, op. cit. note 48.

50. U.N. General Assembly, op. cit. note 48; one third of survivors requiring amputations from CDC, op. cit. note 49. A U.S. employee of the International Rescue Committee became a mine victim in December 1993. In the first two years after the accident, his medical treatment cost $250,000; Christopher S. Wren, "Everywhere, Weapons That Keep on Killing," *New York Times*, 8 October 1995. A staff member of the American Refugee Committee who stepped on a mine in Zaire in October 1995 has incurred medical expenses of $1 million; see CDC, op. cit. note 49; WHO finding from European Parliament, op. cit. note 46.

51. ICRC, "Anti-personnel Mines: An Overview" <http:// www.icrc.org/ icrcnews/>, 1 August 1997; European Parliament, op. cit. note 46; Laurance, op. cit. note 7.

52. Human Rights Watch, op. cit. note 47; U.N. General Assembly, op. cit. note 48; John Battersby, "Gingerly Steps Toward Demining the Globe," *Christian Science Monitor*, 5 October 1994; underfunding from Michael Renner, *Budgeting for Disarmament: The Costs of War and Peace*, Worldwatch Paper 122 (Washington, D.C.: Worldwatch Institute, November 1994); lack of technical progress on demining efforts from U.S. General Accounting Office, "Unexploded Ordnance: A Coordinated Approach to Detection and Clearance Is Needed," GAO/NSIAD-95-197 (Washington, D.C.: GAO, September 1995); demining accident rate from U.N. Department of Humanitarian Affairs, *DHA News*, July/August 1995.

53. U.N. General Assembly, op. cit. note 48.

54. Rana, op. cit. note 7; licensed production from Klare, op. cit. note 18; non-state groups from Stephanie G. Neuman, "The Arms Trade, Military Assistance, and Recent Wars: Change and Continuity," *The Annals of the American Academy*, September 1995, and from Smith, op. cit. note 10.

55. Klare, op. cit. note 18.

56. Goldring, op. cit. note 12.

57. Klare, op. cit. note 20; Klare, op. cit. note 6.

58. Klare, op. cit. note 20; Klare, op. cit. note 6; Klare and Andersen, op. cit. note 3; Mexico from Pierre Thomas and John Ward Anderson, "Mexico Asks U.S. to Track Guns Being Imported by Drug Cartels," *Washington Post*, 5 November 1996, and from Clifford Krauss, "Mexico, Harried Over Drugs, Presses Own Peeve: U.S. Guns," *New York Times*, 19 March 1997.

59. R.T. Naylor, "The Structure and Operation of the Modern Arms Black Market," in Boutwell et al., op. cit. note 2; Table 3 is based on William Reno, "The Business of War in Liberia," *Current History*, May 1996, on Smith, op. cit. note 10, on Rubin, op. cit. note 23, on Neuman, op. cit. note 54, on Cock, op. cit. note 19, on "Still Waiting for Peace," *Economist*, 29 March 1997, on "Demobilizing but Still Divided," *Economist*, 14 September 1996, on Suzanne Daley, "Tensions Threaten Angola's 3-Year Peace," *New York Times*, 1 August 1997, on Eric Berman, *Managing Arms in Peace Processes: Mozambique*, UNIDIR Disarmament and Conflict Resolution Project (New York and Geneva: U.N., 1996), on Jasjit Singh, "Light Weapons and Conflict in Southern Asia," and Tara Kartha, "Southern Asia: The Narcotics and Weapons Linkage," both in Singh, op. cit. note 3, on Klare and Andersen, op. cit. note 3, and on Thomas and Anderson, op. cit. note 58.

60. Latin America and former Yugoslavia from Klare, op. cit. note 6; Algeria and Somalia from Smith, op. cit. note 10; Sierra Leone and Cambodia from Neuman, op. cit. note 54; South Africa from Cock, op. cit. note 19, and from Smith, op. cit. note 10.

61. Estimates of weapons seized from "Albania: Interior Ministry Reports 8 Deaths in Past 24 Hours," Paris AFP in *FBIS Daily Report*, FBIS-EEU-97-083, 24 March 1997, and from "Anarchy in Albania: Collapse of European Collective Security?" *BASIC Papers*, June 1997; bullets from Jane Perlez, "Arrest of Gang Gives Albanians Hope That Chaos Is Ending," *New York Times*, 17 August 1997; "Albania: TV to Broadcast UNICEF Message to Children About Weapons," Paris AFP cited in *FBIS Daily Report*, FBIS-EEU-97-073, 14 March 1997; "Albania: Ministry Laying Mine Fields To Avoid Army Depot Looting," Tirana Radio Tirana Network cited in *FBIS Daily Report*, FBIS-EEU-97-072, 12 March 1997; gun smuggling to neighboring countries from "Albania Village Finds Boom in Gun-Running," *New York Times*, 24 April 1997, and from "Albanian Arms Trafficking Increases," Agence France-Presse, APC electronic computer conference <igc:disarm. armstra>, posted 31 July 1997.

62. Ksenia Gonchar and Peter Lock, "Small Arms and Light Weapons: Russia and the Former Soviet Union," in Boutwell et al., op. cit. note 2; Klare, op. cit. note 20; Sarah Brown, "Modern Tales of the Russian Army," *World Policy Journal*, spring 1997.

63. China from Foster, op. cit. note 35; Pentagon from Gordon Witkin, "Handgun Stealing Made Real Easy," *U.S. News & World Report*, 9 June 1997.

64. Three million firearms from John Mintz, "Amendment Could Bring Flood of Guns Into U.S.," *Washington Post*, 31 July 1997; Michael Brzoska and Herbert Wulf, "Clean Up the World's Glut of Surplus Weapons," *International Herald Tribune*, 5 June 1997; serviceability of arms transferred 40 years ago from Paul F. Pineo and Lora Lumpe, *Recycled Weapons. American Exports of Surplus Arms, 1990–1995* (Washington, D.C.: Arms Sales Monitoring Project, FAS, May 1996).

65. BICC, op. cit. note 13; Brzoska and Wulf, op. cit. note 64; Turkey from Klare, op. cit. note 18.

66. Goldring, op. cit. note 12.

67. Chris Smith, "Light Weapons and Ethnic Conflict in South Asia," in Boutwell et al., op. cit. note 2; estimates of value of weapons can be found in Singh, op. cit. note 3, and in Smith, op. cit. note 10.

68. Singh and Kartha, both op. cit. note 59; Smith, op. cit. note 10.

69. North West Frontier Province, India, and Kashmir from Smith, op. cit. note 67, and from Smith, op. cit. note 10; Tajikistan from Jo L. Husbands, "Controlling Transfers of Light Arms: Linkages to Conflict Processes and Conflict Resolution Strategies," in Boutwell et al., op. cit. note 2; Sri Lanka, Burma, and Algeria from Brzoska and Wulf, op. cit. note 64.

70. Smith, op. cit. note 67; Singh, op. cit. note 59; United Communications Group, "Periscope's USNI Military Database," <http://www.nadn.navy.mil/ MilFacts/weapons/missrock/antiair/w0003205.htm>, last updated 4 March 1996; Daniel McGrory, "CIA Stung by its Stingers," *Electronic Telegraph*, 3 November 1996, <http://www.telegraph.co.uk/et/access?ac= 13924333201&pg=//96/11/3/wstingo3.html>; BICC, op. cit. note 13.

71. Vietnam from Husbands, op. cit. note 69; Central America from Jaramillo, op. cit. note 24; Lebanon and Mozambique from Louise, op. cit. note 37, and from World Bank, "Demobilization and Reintegration of Military Personnel in Africa: The Evidence from Seven Country Case Studies," Discussion Paper, Africa Regional Series, Washington, D.C., October 1993. Table 4 based on Smith, op. cit. note 10, on Klare and Andersen, op. cit. note 3, on "Panamanian Police Seize Arms Destined to Colombian Rebels," *Nando Times*, 9 April 1997, <http://www.nando.net/ newsroom/ntn/world/040997world19_215122.html>, on "Port Said Being Used for Arms Trafficking from Central America," *El Panama America* (Panama City), cited in *FBIS Daily Report*, FBIS-LAT-96-225, 16 November 1996, on "Ex-Guerrilleros Se Acusan de Venta de Armamento," *El Diario de Hoy*, 25 February 1997, on "Guardado y Samayoa Son Profugos de la Justicia en Nicaragua," *El Diario de Hoy*, 25 February 1997, on Howard LaFranchi, "Mexicans Too Have a Problem: Awash in U.S. Guns," *Christian Science Monitor*, 20 April 1997, on "80 Killed in Kenya Clashes," *New York Times*, 28 March 1997, on Cock, op. cit. note 19, and on Latham, op. cit. note 44.

72. Secondhand markets from Naylor, op. cit. note 59, and from Smith, op. cit. note 10.

73. BICC, *Conversion Survey 1996: Global Disarmament, Demilitarization and Demobilization* (New York: Oxford University Press, 1996); U.S. Department of Defense, Office of the Undersecretary of Defense (Comptroller), *National Defense Budget Estimates for FY 1996* (Washington, D.C.: National Technical Information Service, March 1995); Howard W. French, "Liberian Militias Lay Down Arms and Raise Hopes," *New York Times*, 27 January 1997; *International Security Digest*, October 1996. Table 5 is based on BICC, op. cit. this note, on U.N. Security Council, "Twenty-Second Progress Report of the Secretary-General on the U.N. Observer Mission in Liberia," S/1997/237, 19

March 1997, and on "Army Spokesman Says Over 60 Percent of PACs Demobilized," *La Republica* (Guatemala City) in *FBIS Daily Report*, FBIS-LAT-96-203, 16 October 1996.

74. BICC, "Demobilization and Reintegration," <http://bicc.uni-bonn.de/demobil/demobil.html>, last updated 4 June 1997.

75. Kees Kingma and Vanessa Sayers, *Demobilization in the Horn of Africa*, BICC Brief 4 (Bonn: BICC, June 1995).

76. Rioting in Mozambique from Peter Batchelor, "Disarmament, Small Arms, and Intra-State Conflict: The Case of Southern Africa," in Smith et al., op. cit. note 10; desertions in Angola from U.N. Security Council, "Progress Report of the Secretary-General on the United Nations Angola Verification Mission (UNAVEM III)," S/1997/438, 5 June 1997; BICC, op. cit. note 73; N.J. Colletta and M. Kostner, "War-to-Peace Transition in Mozambique: The Provincial Reintegration Support Program," *Findings* (World Bank newsletter), July 1997.

77. BICC, op. cit. note 73.

78. Mbeki quoted in Andrew Selsky, "Angola Peace Plan on Track," Associated Press, 8 January 1997; BICC, op. cit. note 73; Kingma and Sayers, op. cit. note 75.

79. Batchelor, op. cit. note 76; BICC, op. cit. note 73.

80. BICC, op. cit. note 73; Larry Rohter, "Destitute Ex-Contras Demand U.S. Aid," *New York Times*, 24 October 1996; Paulo Wrobel, *Managing Arms in Peace Processes: Nicaragua and El Salvador*, UNIDIR Disarmament and Conflict Resolution Project (New York and Geneva: U.N., 1996); *Central America Update*, 21 March 1997; "Nicaragua: Aleman Stresses 28 February Deadline for Laying Down Weapons," *Managua La Prensa* in *FBIS Daily Report*, FBIS-LAT-97-034, 18 February 1997; "Nicaragua: Defense Minister Comments on Talks with Rearmed Groups," Managua Canal Dos Television in *FBIS Daily Report*, FBIS-LAT-97-039, 23 February 1997; "Cinco Jefes de 3-80 Abandonan Dialogo," *Notifax*, 18 April 1997; "Armados Amenazan Poblado," *Notifax*, 16 April 1997, <http://www.notifax.com/>.

81. Cock, op. cit. note 19; Batchelor, op. cit. note 76.

82. Batchelor, op. cit. note 76.

83. "Still Waiting for Peace," op.cit. note 59; U.N. Security Council, op. cit. note 76; Suzanne Daley, "Ex-Rebels Adrift in an Angola Without a War," *New York Times*, 17 June 1997; Suzanne Daley, "Tensions Threaten Angola's 3-Year Peace," *New York Times*, 1 August 1997; Barbara Crossette, "U.N. Puts Strong Sanctions on an Angola Rebel Force," *New York Times*, 29 August 1997; Peta Thornycroft, "SA Supplying Arms to Unita," *Weekly Mail &*

Guardian (South Africa), 20 June 1997, <http://wn.apc.org/wmail/issues/970620/NEWS2.html>.

84. Gallik, op. cit. note 21; Michael Specter, "Yeltsin's Plan to Cut Military Touches a Nerve," *New York Times*, 28 July 1997; William M. Arkin, "Russia's Port-a-Nukes," *The Nation*, 29 September 1997.

85. Benjamin S. Lambeth, "An Ailing Army Needs Our Help" (Op-Ed), *New York Times*, 28 February 1995; "Russian Army May Be Close to Collapse, a Study Finds," *New York Times*, 17 February 1997; Specter, op. cit. note 84.

86. Council for Foreign and Defense Policy from "Russian Army May Be Close to Collapse ...", op. cit. note 85; better support for Interior Ministry troops from "'Demoralisiert und Zerrüttet'," *Der Spiegel* (Germany), no. 11/1997; Rokhlin from Katrina van den Heuvel and Stephen F. Cohen, "The Other Russia," *The Nation*, 11/18 August 1997.

87. Smith, op. cit. note 10.

88. Laurance, op. cit. note 7.

89. The discussion in the text and Table 6 are based on the following sources: Zawels et al., op. cit. note 2; Wrobel, op. cit. note 80; Laurance, op. cit. note 7; Batchelor, op. cit. note 76; Berman, op. cit. note 59; Smith, op. cit. note 10; Daley, op. cit. note 44; Clement Adibe, *Managing Arms in Peace Processes: Somalia*, UNIDIR Disarmament and Conflict Resolution Project (New York and Geneva: U.N., 1995); David Cox, "Peacekeeping and Disarmament: Peace Agreements, Security Council Mandates, and the Disarmament Experience," in Zawels, op. cit. note 2; Jianwei Wang, *Managing Arms in Peace Processes: Cambodia*, UNIDIR Disarmament and Conflict Resolution Project (New York and Geneva: U.N., 1996); Yvan Cohen, "Guns-R-Us Culture In Cambodia Slowly Yields to Rule Of Law," *Christian Science Monitor*, 6 March 1997.

90. Laurance, op. cit. note 7; Batchelor, op. cit. note 76; Smith, op. cit. note 10; Fred Tanner, "Consensual Versus Coercive Disarmament," in Zawels, op. cit. note 2.

91. Smith, op. cit. note 10.

92. Need for swift disarmament from Sverre Lodgaard, "Demobilization and Disarmament: Experiences to Date," *UNIDIR Newsletter*, no. 32, 1996; reasons for reneging and the tradeoffs between consensual and coercive disarmament are discussed by Tanner, op. cit. note 90.

93. Table 7 is based on the following sources: Laurance, op. cit. note 7; Armadeo Cabrera, "Arranca de Nuevo Campaña Bienes por Armas de Fuego," *La Prensa Grafica*, 6 March 1997; "Mas de 500 Armas Recolectadas el Fin de Semana," *La Nacion*, 8 April 1997, <http://www.nacion.co.cr>;

"Urgen Ley para Control de Armas de Fuego," *El Diario de Hoy*, 3 April 1997, <http://www.elsalvador.com>; Douglas Farah, "Cash for Cached Weapons," *Washington Post*, 1 November 1996; Daley, op. cit. note 44; "Gun Control Report Due to be Studied by Committee," *Otago Daily Times* (New Zealand), 1 July 1997; Brazil and Berry, "Australia's Answer ...," op. cit. note 34; "Most Australian Gun Owners Have Handed in Guns," Reuters, 26 August 1997, APC electronic computer conference <igc:disarm.armstra>, posted 29 August 1997; David Elias, "Farewell to Arms, Gun by Gun," *The Age Online*, 20 September 1977 <http://www.theage.com.au:80/daily/970920/news/ news1.htm/>; "600,000 Guns Turned in During Australian Gun Amnesty," 30 September 1997, <http://www.nando.net/newsroom/ntn/world/ 093097/world16_20836.html>.

94. Laurance, op. cit. note 7; Lodgaard, op. cit. note 92; Batchelor, op. cit. note 76.

95. Lodgaard, op. cit. note 92; amnesty programs from "Prime Minister Offers Pardon for 'Unlawful' Firearms," Maseru Radio Lesotho in *FBIS Daily Report*, FBIS-AFR-96-211, 30 October 1996, from "Sri Lanka Sets Arms Deadline," *World News*, 2 February 1997, <http://wire.AP.org>, and from United Kingdom Home Office, "22,939 Guns Collected in the Firearms Amnesty," Press Release 235/96, 23 July 1996, <http://www.coi.gov.uk/ coi/depts/GHO/coi0775c.ok>, viewed 29 May 1997.

96. Karp, op. cit. note 2.

97. Klare, op. cit. note 6.

98. Susannah L. Dyer and Natalie J. Goldring, "Analysing Policy Proposals to Limit Light Weapons Transfers," in Singh, op. cit. note 3.

99. Stephen Kinzer, "Nobel Peace Laureates Draft a Plan to Govern Arms Trade," *New York Times*, 6 September 1995; "Speech by Dr. Oscar Arias at Capitol Hill Symposium," Washington, D.C., 15 December 1995, APC electronic computer conference <igc:disarm.armstra>, posted 19 December 1995; "Nobel Laureates' International Code of Conduct on Arms Transfers," retrieved from BASIC Web site, <http://www.igc.apc.org/basic/code_itl.htm>.

100. Michael S. Lelyveld, "Bill Backed by Rights Groups Has Weapons Exporters up in Arms," *Journal of Commerce*, 28 April 1997; "Banning Arms for Dictators" (editorial), *New York Times*, 20 June 1997; Jordana Friedman, Campaign Coordinator, The Year 2000 Campaign to Redirect World Military Spending to Human Development, "Endorsement, Media, and Legislative Update," 1 August 1997.

101. "Arias Introduces Code of Conduct," *Arms Trade News*, June 1997; "Banning Arms for Dictators," op. cit. note 100; BASIC, "Codes of Conduct on Arms Transfers: An Opportunity for the United States and its European Allies to Work Together," <http://www.igc.apc.org/basic/basic_sw.htm>, viewed 25 September 1997; Organization on Security and Cooperation in Europe (OSCE), "Criteria on Conventional Arms Transfers," November 1993, <http://www.igc.apc.org/basic/oscecode.htm>; Britain from Alan Wheatley, "Britain Tightens Curbs on Arms Exports," <http://www.yahoo.com/headlines/970728/international/stories/weapons_2.html>, 28 July 1997.

102. Karp, op. cit. note 2; Laurance, op. cit. note 7.

103. Klare, op. cit. note 6; Goldring, op. cit. note 12; Lora Lumpe, "Preliminary Policy Options for Monitoring/Restricting Exports of Light Arms," Federation of American Scientists Web site, <http://www.fas.org/light_weapons/light2.htm#head6>, viewed 28 May 1997.

104. "Jamaica Says U.S. Agrees to Regional Gun Talks," Reuter, 20 March 1997, retrieved from San Jose Mercury Web site, <http://www.merc.com/stories/cgi/story.cgi?id=2024555-87c>; Mexico from LaFranchi, op. cit. note 71; the OAS agreement is known as the "Draft Inter-American Convention Against the Illicit Manufacturing of and Trafficking in Firearms, Ammunition, Explosives and Other Related Materials"; see U.N., op. cit. note 4; Central America from Sarah Meek, "United Nations Report on Firearms Regulation," Institute for Security Studies Occasional Paper No. 23, June 1997, APC electronic computer conference <igc:disarm.armstra>, posted 4 August 1997; tripartite agreement from Batchelor, op. cit. note 76; South Africa-Mozambique agreement from Cock, op. cit. note 19, from "Police in Mozambique Destroy Cache of Arms," New York Times, 12 August 1997, and from Alex Belida, "SAF/Mozambique," Voice of America, 12 August 1997 [NEB/BEL/PCF], <gopher://gopher.voa.gov:70/00/newswire/tue/SAF_-_MOZAMBIQUE>; Europe from "The EU Programme for Preventing and Combatting Illicit Trafficking in Conventional Arms," International Security Digest, July 1997.

105. Naylor, op. cit. note 59.

106. Katharine Q. Seelye, "Heston Asserts Gun Ownership Is Nation's Highest Right," New York Times, 12 September 1997.

107. Problem of lack of restrictions in one country affecting other countries from Sarah Brady, "Our Nation's Claim to Shame: U.N. Study Finds U.S. is a Leading Source of Firearms for International Gun Smugglers," press release, Handgun Control, Inc., Washington, D.C., 5 May 1997.

108. Institute for Defense and Disarmament Studies (IDDS), Arms Control Reporter 1997 (Cambridge, MA), section 708.A.

109. U.S. Campaign to Ban Landmines, Landmines Update, June 1997, APC electronic computer conference <igc:disarm.armstra>, posted 22 June 1997; Raymond Bonner, "How a Group of Outsiders Moved Nations to Ban Land Mines, " New York Times, 20 September 1997; number of countries taking anti-mine measures calculated from U.S. Campaign to Ban Landmines,

Landmines Update, July 1996, APC electronic computer conference <igc:disarm.armstra>, from ICRC, <http://www.icrc.org./icrcnews/490e.htm>, viewed 28 May 1997, from Stuart Maslen, ICRC, Geneva, fax to Daniel Schwartz, Worldwatch Institute, 15 July 1997, and from IDDS, op. cit. note 108.

110. ICRC, <http://www.icrc.org/icrcnews/482e.htm>; U.S. Campaign to Ban Landmines, "Final Declaration for the Brussels Conference on Anti-Personnel Landmines," APC electronic computer conference <igc:disarm. armstra>, posted 1 July 1997; U.S. Campaign to Ban Landmines, "Information on Oslo Conference," APC electronic computer conference <igc:disarm.armstra>, posted 21 August 1997; Raymond Bonner, "Land Mine Treaty Takes Final Form Over U.S. Dissent," *New York Times*, 18 September 1997.

111. Tim Weiner, "U.S. Is Wary of Ban on Land Mines," *New York Times*, 17 June 1997; James Bennet, "U.S. Agrees to Join Talks on Banning Some Mines," *New York Times*, 19 August 1997; U.S. Campaign to Ban Landmines, "More Detail on Proposed US Exception," APC electronic computer conference <igc:disarm.armstra>, posted 19 August 1997; Bonner, op.cit. note 110; Steven Lee Myers, "Clinton Says Land Mine Ban Could Endanger U.S. Troops," *New York Times*, 18 September 1997.

112. U.S. Campaign to Ban Landmines, *Ban Treaty News*, 16 September 1997, APC electronic computer conference <igc:disarm.armstra>.

PUBLICATION ORDER FORM

_____ *State of the World:* $13.95
The annual book used by journalists, activists, scholars, and policymakers worldwide to get a clear picture of the environmental problems we face.

_____ *Vital Signs:* $12.00
The book of trends that are shaping our future in easy to read graph and table format, with a brief commentary on each trend.

_____ WORLD WATCH **magazine subscription: $20.00 (international airmail $35.00)**
Stay abreast of global environmental trends and issues with our award-winning, eminently readable bimonthly magazine.

_____ **Worldwatch Library: $30.00 (international subscribers $45)**
Receive *State of the World* and all six Worldwatch Papers as they are released during the calendar year.

_____ **Worldwatch Database Disk Subscription: $89.00**
Contains global agricultural, energy, economic, environmental, social, and military indicators from all current Worldwatch publications including this Paper. Includes a mid-year update, and *Vital Signs* and *State of the World* as they are published. Can be used with Lotus 1-2-3, Quattro Pro, Excel, SuperCalc and many other spreadsheets. **Check one:** _____ **IBM-compatible or** _____ **Macintosh**

_____ **Worldwatch Papers—See complete list on following page**
Single copy: $5.00 • 2–5: $4.00 ea. • 6–20: $3.00 ea. • 21 or more: $2.00 ea. (Call Director of Communication, at (202) 452-1999, for discounts on larger orders.)

$4.00 Shipping and Handling *($8.00 outside North America)*

_____ **TOTAL**

Make check payable to Worldwatch Institute
1776 Massachusetts Ave., NW, Washington, DC 20036-1904 USA

Enclosed is my check or purchase order for U.S. $_____

☐ AMEX ☐ VISA ☐ MasterCard _____
                              Card Number   Expiration Date

_____
name   **daytime phone #**

_____
address

_____
city   **state**   **zip/country**

phone: (202) 452-1999   fax: (202) 296-7365   e-mail: wwpub@worldwatch.org
website: www.worldwatch.org

☐ **Send me a brochure of all Worldwatch publications.**

Worldwatch Papers

No. of Copies

Worldwatch Papers by Michael Renner:

_____137. **Small Arms, Big Impact: The Next Challenge of Disarmament** by Michael Renner

_____122. **Budgeting for Disarmament: The Costs of War and Peace** by Michael Renner

_____114. **Critical Juncture: The Future of Peacekeeping** by Michael Renner

_____104. **Jobs in a Sustainable Economy** by Michael Renner

_____ 96. **Swords Into Plowshares: Converting to a Peace Economy** by Michael Renner

_____136. **The Agricultural Link: How Environmental Deterioration Could Disrupt Economic Progress** by Lester R. Brown

_____135. **Recycling Organic Waste: From Urban Pollutant to Farm Resource** by Gary Gardner

_____134. **Getting the Signals Right: Tax Reform to Protect the Environment and the Economy** by David Malin Roodman

_____133. **Paying the Piper: Subsidies, Politics, and the Environment** by David Malin Roodman

_____132. **Dividing the Waters: Food Security, Ecosystem Health, and the New Politics of Scarcity** by Sandra Postel

_____131. **Shrinking Fields: Cropland Loss in a World of Eight Billion** by Gary Gardner

_____130. **Climate of Hope: New Strategies for Stabilizing the World's Atmosphere** by Christopher Flavin and Odil Tunali

_____129. **Infecting Ourselves: How Environmental and Social Disruptions Trigger Disease** by Anne E. Platt

_____128. **Imperiled Waters, Impoverished Future: The Decline of Freshwater Ecosystems** by Janet N. Abramovitz

_____127. **Eco-Justice: Linking Human Rights and the Environment** by Aaron Sachs

_____126. **Partnership for the Planet: An Environmental Agenda for the United Nations** by Hilary F. French

_____125. **The Hour of Departure: Forces That Create Refugees and Migrants** by Hal Kane

_____124. **A Building Revolution: How Ecology and Health Concerns Are Transforming Construction** by David Malin Roodman and Nicholas Lenssen

_____123. **High Priorities: Conserving Mountain Ecosystems and Cultures** by Derek Denniston

_____121. **The Next Efficiency Revolution: Creating a Sustainable Materials Economy** by John E. Young and Aaron Sachs

_____120. **Net Loss: Fish, Jobs, and the Marine Environment** by Peter Weber

_____119. **Powering the Future: Blueprint for a Sustainable Electricity Industry** by Christopher Flavin and Nicholas Lenssen

_____118. **Back on Track: The Global Rail Revival** by Marcia D. Lowe

_____117. **Saving the Forests: What Will It Take?** by Alan Thein Durning

_____116. **Abandoned Seas: Reversing the Decline of the Oceans** by Peter Weber

_____115. **Global Network: Computers in a Sustainable Society** by John E. Young

_____113. **Costly Tradeoffs: Reconciling Trade and the Environment** by Hilary F. French

_____111. **Empowering Development: The New Energy Equation** by Nicholas Lenssen

_____110. **Gender Bias: Roadblock to Sustainable Development** by Jodi L. Jacobson

_____106. **Nuclear Waste: The Problem That Won't Go Away** by Nicholas Lenssen

_____105. **Shaping Cities: The Environmental and Human Dimensions** by Marcia D. Lowe

_____102. **Women's Reproductive Health: The Silent Emergency** by Jodi L. Jacobson

_____101. **Discarding the Throwaway Society** by John E. Young

_____100. **Beyond the Petroleum Age: Designing a Solar Economy** by Christopher Flavin and Nicholas Lenssen

_____ 97. **The Global Politics of Abortion** by Jodi L. Jacobson

_____**Total copies (transfer number to order form on previous page)**